Around *The* WORLD In *Eighty* Martinis

THE LOGBOOK OF A REMARKABLE VOYAGE
UNDERTAKEN BY
GUSTAV TEMPLE & VIC DARKWOOD

4th

4TH ESTATE • LONDON

Acknowledgements

Messrs Temple & Darkwood would like to extend a cordial slap on the shoulder to the following coves, without whom this circumnavigation would not have been plausible:

JAKE CLARK	NICK DAVIES
MARIA TERESA GAVAZZI	ROBIN HARVIE
JAN HASSAN	CHIEKO INOUE
ANDREW LAMB	TONY LYONS
ALAN MURPHY	MASAKI NAKATAKE
FIONA SALTER	DAVID SAXBY
SUSAN SMITH	NICOLA SOUTHIN

First published in Great Britain in 2003 by Fourth Estate. A Division of HarperCollins Publishers
77–85 Fulham Palace Road, London W6 8JB. www.4thestate.com

Copyright © Gavin Clark & Nicholas Jolly 2003

The right of Gavin Clark and Nicholas Jolly to be identified as the authors of this work has been asserted by them in accordance with the Copyright, Designs and Patents Act 1988.

A catalogue record for this book is available from the British Library. ISBN: 0-00-71620-5

Designed by M2, London. Original illustrations and map by Tony McSweeney.

Printed by Scotprint, Haddington.

Contents

Prologue

On a wet Wednesday in November at the beginning of the 21st century, Gustav Temple and Vic Darkwood were seated at their usual spot in the Smoking Room of the Sheridan Club on St James's Street, London. They were closely observing the progress of two raindrops running down a window pane, having placed a wager on which particular drop would be the first to reach the window sill.

In the cluster of leather armchairs behind them, a heated discussion was taking place on the nature of foreign travel. Temple and Darkwood, normally among the most garrulous participants in Smoking Room badinage, were trying to remain as inconspicuous as possible, for today was the date of annual renewal of membership to the Sheridan Club. The sum, though not exorbitant, was far beyond the means of either of these two rum coves, since they were both what is known in tradesmen's circles as "borassic lint". A combination of Temple's obsession with the baccarat tables and Darkwood's chronic dipsomania had resulted in yet another year of bitter disappointment and financial ruin. They discreetly lent an ear to the conversation behind them, in the desperate hope of finding a way out of their current predicament.

"Absolute tommyrot!" Wilkinson was saying to Arbuthnot. "Foreign travel does absolutely nothing to broaden the mind. It is a form of medicine peculiar to our age, designed to treat the nervous apoplexy of the working man."

"I couldn't agree more," Harkinshaw piped in. "Any man in possession of a half decent library and a comfortable armchair has no need to set foot outside of his rooms in search of experience."

"Indeed," said Wilkinson. "For the gentleman, foreign travel is nothing but a series of indignities – gastronomic, lavatorial and linguistic. How, for instance, is one to communicate with all the required porters, innkeepers and bordello operatives, in the complete absence of a common tongue? Imagine someone like our friends Mr Temple and Mr Darkwood trying to negotiate their way across, say, India. They can't even get to the north side of Piccadilly without meeting some incident."

At this juncture Gustav Temple joined the men at the fireplace. "Gentlemen, allow me to differ. The incident to which you refer was entirely the fault of an assistant in Fortnum & Mason, who allowed the ocelot I was purchasing to escape from its cage and make a dash for Bond Street. Furthermore, Mr Darkwood has been known to cross the river on occasion."

"Being carried on a stretcher hardly counts," Wilkinson snorted.

"The only way to travel is with one's eyes fixed on the stars," the voice of Vic Darkwood boomed from behind the wings of a Queen Anne leather armchair. He levered himself up, with the difficulty of a man devoted to the twin pursuits of drinking port and sitting still, and lumbered over to the group at the fireplace. "With the combination of Mr Temple's *savoir faire* and my manual dexterity," he continued, clinging on to the mantelpiece for support, "we would not only be able to complete a voyage into foreign climes, but we could cross every one of the world's five continents."

"Fiddlesticks!" said Wilkinson. "A large amount of money says you couldn't!"

"Mm," said Arbuthnot, observing the frayed lapels of Darkwood's only suit, "something tells me that, with enough incentive, they probably could."

"Are you prepared to put twenty thousand pounds behind your opinion?" Wilkinson asked him, raising his eyebrows in a rather pompous fashion.

"That all depends on how difficult you want to make it for them," Arbuthnot replied, with the disdainful arch of a single eyebrow.

Newspapers were quickly folded, brandy glasses were filled, and old Buddlesworth was awoken. Temple and Darkwood were asked to wait outside the door while the men thrashed out the conditions attendant on the wager and the amount to be received by the winning backers.

Presently, Temple and Darkwood were ushered back into the Smoking Room. "If you are back in this room within a reasonable period of time," Arbuthnot solemnly announced, "having crossed all five continents of the world using a different form of transport for every country visited, I stand to win forty thousand pounds, half of which I am willing to advance to you for use as travel expenses and to renew your membership of the Sheridan Club. Mr Wilkinson has very kindly offered to loan you Masaki, his Japanese valet's cousin, who will accompany you as an adjudicator. If you fail on any of the counts, Mr Wilkinson will win forty thousand pounds and you will return to certain ignominy and the termination of your membership to the club. Do you accept the conditions?"

Temple and Darkwood, unable to foresee any such sum ever coming their way again, accepted the wager without reservation.

Europe

WELCOME TO FRANCE. WE WILL TRY TO BE NICE TO YOU!*

A✱S.

*BUT WE CANNOT MAKE ANY PROMISES.

451

Limoges, France, 7th November

What on earth have we got ourselves in to? I was unfortunately three-sheets-to-the-wind when we agreed to embark on this ludicrous caper. Indeed, if I had been in possession of a more becalmed liver I would have surely declined such an imbecilic proposal out of hand. As it is we find ourselves having "signed on the dotted", contracted into certain calamity. "South of the river" is one thing, but "abroad" is quite another.

It is 11.35am and we are sitting on the edge of the bandstand in the Jardin D'Orsay, Limoges, whilst Masaki has gone in pursuit of accommodation, victuals and our first martinis of the day. I hope he returns soon. We are both exhausted by our ordeal. Despite our recently acquired wealth, Gustav has the look of a man who has foreseen the manner of his own death and is not entirely pleased by the vision. I will be very surprised if either of us makes it as far as Zagreb, let alone the full itinerary.

In order to soften the blow of our initial foray onto the Continent, Gustav alighted on the idea of approaching our old chum "Spritely" Hardcourt, who owns a small four-seater hovercraft, which he keeps in an old barn just outside Hurstpierpoint. Spritely was delighted to oblige and, moreover, to receive the £2200 that we had to shelve out for the privilege of travelling in his chariot du vent (as he likes to call it). What is more, he readily agreed (for an extra £400) to pick us up directly from the front door of the club. To bypass any unnecessary attention from the local constabulary we decided to set off in the early hours of the morning. I have to confess to feeling rather emotional as we bid adieu to Arbuthnot and Wilkinson, and glided down the Haymarket towards our appointment with the unknown.

The hovercraft turned out to be a very handy piece of equipment indeed, allowing us as it did to travel directly down the M23 to Brighton (where we arrived by 3.30am) and embark on the channel crossing all in one fell swoop. It was also jolly useful in circumventing time-consuming petty bureaucracy such as customs and excise, and passport control. It did however present us with some limitations. Due to the shortage of space in the cabin we were hard put to cram in the luggage, and, so, to avoid water damage to our leather portmanteaux and travel trunks, we were forced to consign Masaki to the indignities of the roof rack. Gustav maintained that this was not unduly cruel as it would serve to "toughen him up a bit" for the rigours of the many adventures that lay ahead, but I have to admit that by the time we reached the French coast at Fécamp and checked our "load" he did look quite astonishingly blue in the lips, with salt crystals encrusting his eyebrows and side whiskers. "Not long now, old chap. Just another 4 hours to Limoges," I reassured him. It might have been my imagination, but I thought I caught a slight hint of resentment in his eyes. I do hope he is not the sort of fellow to harbour a grudge.

Fécamp is a quaint little fishing port with a good selection of restaurants. To save time and the bother of untying all those difficult knots, we left Masaki in situ for the brief two hours that it took to locate and consume a hearty breakfast, and to visit the imposing Palace of Alexandre Le Grand. It is here that the liqueur Benedictine is distilled and we wasted no time making our way to the shop and stocked up on half a dozen bottles of the sacred elixir. On returning to the hover we brought Masaki round with a goodly snifter and fed him a couple of warm croissants, which seemed to raise his spirits considerably. The morning sun had thawed him out a bit and his chin was set with renewed determination. I must say I admired his pluck.

The final hours to Limoges were unremarkable enough. Gustav and I wrapped ourselves in travel kilims and indulged in a few drops of laudanum to make the journey pass more pleasantly. Gustav had suggested Limoges as a destination partly because of geography, it being roughly halfway to our next destination of Barcelona, and partly because he was curious to visit the place of origin of Limoges enamelware, as he is the proud owner of a rather fine collection of 16th century enamel funerary urns. He was further encouraged by Spritely's claim that he knew of a charming little bordello in the town run by a pair of albino sisters. Must say it all sounds très exotique and not a little séduisant.

Alas, all this will have to wait for tomorrow. For the time being we are far too shell-shocked by the whole notion of travel and its attendant discomforts. I can now see Masaki making his way back towards us across the gravel carrying aloft a tray of Martinis. Maybe "abroad" will not turn out to be so bloody after all.

ARTS & CULTURE:
THE MUSÉE NIVEN

IF ONE IS taking the traditional route through the Massif Central, one could do considerably worse than make a brief detour to Nice, if only to visit this charming little museum. Every French town in has its Musée Niven, to honour the actor's decision to live out his final years in France. This one has the usual collection of *ephemera Nivena*: moustaches preserved in amber, cravats, dinner jackets etc. But the real pièce de résistance is the *Chambre des Anecdotes*. Each of these five rooms contains recordings of Niven's legendary anecdotes, played through hidden speakers at the touch of a button. In the final room, Niven's longest anecdote ever is played. It involves a Martini glass, several olives, a large laundry basket and Errol Flynn. After 45 minutes, the anecdote trails off into poignant and moving silence.

MUSÉE NIVEN
Rue des Picateurs, 11, Nice 39216
Open 11am-6pm daily. Entry fee € 8.

TRUBSHAWE'S
Oddification Rating
★ ★ ★ ☆ ☆

The Wasp Waist

FEW NATIONS CAN compete with the French when it comes to effete affectations in the realms of facial hair, perfumery and sartorial matters.

Usually a competent tailor can be relied upon to work miracles in concealing the inadequacies of a fellow's physique, but in France a gentleman who wishes to cut a dash will employ the additional services of a tightly laced corset to give his body that certain extra *je ne sais quoi*.

Through prolongued use of a reinforced whale-bone bodice, this chap has trained his waist to an elegant girth of 19 inches in order to oddify his torso into an artwork of considerable sculptural beauty.

RESTAURANT:
LE SYNÆSTHESIE

THIS RESTAURANT IN Riberac describes its style as French Symbolist and Chef Paul Gaché has taken the symbolist preoccupation with synaesthesia as the starting point for his highly innovative cuisine. No actual food appears on the menu, instead the guests are expected to "experience" the taste of the courses using their other senses (touch, sight, hearing etc). For example, one of the hors d'oeuvres simply reads *Le Couleur Bleu*. A guest who orders this will be presented with a small blue card which must be stared at intently for a few seconds. The resultant 'taste' is something akin to a chicken liver paté. For a main course try *Les Cloches Sonnant Fort* which entails three waiters robustly clanging old school bells next to the table for 15 minutes or so. To my mind this had a spicy beef flavour with a distinct dijon sauce accompaniment. For pudding an adventurous diner may decide to go for *Un petit oiseau à l'intérieur de sa chemise*. Who would have thought that a budgerigar being released inside one's shirt could taste so uncannily like the lightest of crèmes brûlées?

Highly recommended ★ ★ ★ ★ ☆

PARLONS FRANCAIS

FRENCH IS A richly complex language full of subtle nuance and hidden meaning. For linguistic accuracy, the following everyday phrases should be delivered with an exaggerated shrug and a lugubrious raising of the eyebrows.

Yes, we are very pleased to welcome you to our humble little hotel.
Oui?

No, we do not provide any lavatorial facilities other than that filthy hole in the ground.
Oui, c'est tout.

I'm afraid to say we are fresh out of Lapsang Souchong. Is there anything else I can offer you?
Pas du thé.

It is greatly to our discredit that we are not able to offer a more substantial breakfast to our honoured English visitors.
Un croissant?

Would you be so kind as to vacate your table, because an old man in a beret wishes to use it for a lengthy coughing fit.
Au revoir, messieurs.

Unfortunately we do not sell cigarettes made with a delicious blend of Turkish and Virginia tobacco.
Gauloises, monsieur?

Nouveau En LIMOGES

Landlady 'Anglaise'

★ **Photo genuine**
Service discrete
Visites à l'hotel
Ambience authentique
du 'B&B' anglaise

Chatiments offrés aux
'naughty gentlemen' pour:

★ Utilisez trop papier du toilette;

★ Revenir aux B&B trop tard;

★ Faire trop de bruit sur l'escalier;

★ Demander les choses 'fancy'
pour le petit dejeuner;

★ Abusir les 'tea-making facilities'
dans le chambre

Vous aimez les grands portions monsieur? **08564 232468**

Barcelona, Spain, 12th November

SPANISH COVES

I write this upon a handsome oak escritoire in the Presidential Suite of the Hotel Esplendido in Barcelona. The reason for choosing the single most expensive room we could find in this fair city was to atone for the rather unpleasant journey we were subjected to in coming here from France. The trouble began in Limoges. If the French can be described as somewhat surly and brusque in their manner, then the Limogese must be coveting the title of most impertinent citizens of the land.

"We should like to commandeer a hansom carriage," I explained to a gendarme directing traffic at a busy roundabout, "to transport us to your southern European cousins. Would you be so kind as to assist us?"

The fellow replied with a barrage of what sounded like rather unparliamentary language and waved us away. We were reluctant to squander our single permitted taxicab journey (at least for the purposes of making the actual voyage as opposed to recreational trips), but as Masaki pointed out, the more exotic forms of travel would in all likelihood present themselves to us further afield. The shrewd Oriental was right in principle, but unfortunately the taxicab is not a familiar form of transport in the Midi region of France, and we were forced to broaden the scope of our enquiries.

The result could be interpreted by some as 'exotic', but to Victor and myself, the fortnight's journey into northern Spain in the back of a donkey and cart was nothing short of a travesty. The driver was a typically surly peasant with poor dentistry and even poorer personal hygiene. We made Masaki ride in front with him while Victor and myself settled among the vegetables in the back of the cart.

I lay back on a sack of onions watching the endless treetops passing overhead and dreamed of Monte Carlo. I pictured myself in the Salle de Jeu, hurling vast quantities of Arbuthnot's cash on the Roulette table to the thrilled cries of an ecstatic crowd. It was not until we reached Perpignan that I discovered we were not to pass anywhere near Monte Carlo.

The French, we surmised, were sadly lacking in the snobbery we had expected of them. Everywhere we were received with gruff nods and non-committal grunts, and the lavatorial facilities were hardly aristocratic. We decided that the sophisticated people must all live exclusively in Paris and Monaco, and we had visited neither in our haste to fulfil this ludicrous wager.

Spain, however, turned out to be a revelation. We had prepared ourselves for roving gypsies with daggers, bulls running through the streets and appalling drainage, but compared to France, Spain was a paragon of civility and hygiene. Our suite at the Esplendido has three, or possibly four bathrooms. The fourth we presume to be intended for infants, since it contains a miniature bathtub at ankle level. Masaki has designated it for use as an undergarment laundry to which Victor, mysteriously, is unwilling to contribute.

The Corby Trouser Press is the C360 model, which greatly excites me for it means I shall be able to press all 17 of my pairs of flannels in one evening. I was just about to insert the first pair, however, when I discovered to my horror that Victor had got there first and used the Corby to chargrill a pair of gammon steaks he had brought with him.

The Spanish are a curious people. Impeccably groomed in a rather Bourgeois sort of fashion, they devote much of their day to ambling up and down the extensive boulevards of their city. We joined in with their ambling and found it entirely to our taste: a slow, gentle activity with no purpose whatsoever. There is little sign of anyone working, although it is true that the menfolk disappear into tall buildings during the afternoon, but this is presumably to take an afternoon snooze. The womenfolk then set about washing the steps of their dwellings. All in all, it seems an efficient and well-balanced society.

We wondered how such eccentrics as Salvador Dalí, could have emerged from so sedate and orderly a community, and our first nocturnal stroll furnished us with an answer. There are several small taverns deep within the bowels of Barcelona where the sole victual purveyed is Absenta, or Absinth. Nowhere in France had our long-awaited communion with La fee vert been offered to us, but here it seemed that Dionysus was smiling upon us. The decrepit old hostelry we discovered seemed to have been lifted entirely from a tableau by Degas. The dusty bottles behind the bar all contained variants of Absinth, and every glass in the establishment was filled with the pearly green mixture.

By the time we departed, we were left in no doubt as to the origins of Surrealism. The taxi driver was so impressed by Victor's impromptu attempt to recite dada poetry in Spanish that he took us on a scenic route back to the hotel, via some outlying villages in the mountains surrounding Barcelona.

And now I must begin to reinstate my flannels into my portmanteau, for tomorrow we must locate an able seaman to navigate us across the Mediterranean.

On crest of the waves: Sports

British groups triumph: INSIDE

SPANIARD CAUGHT ON MALLORCA

Palma, 12th June. A man has been arrested by Mallorcan police on a charge of being 'Spanish'.

JUAN JOSÉ JIMENEZ de la Rueda, 19, of Alcudia, was apprehended by the Civil Guard as he motored home on his scooter. His clothes, hair, skin tone and general demeanour immediately aroused suspicion in the local police force. Major Henry Burghley-Wittington, chief superintendent of Mallorca's Civil Guard, is heading the case.

"My officers raised their eyebrows when Mr Jimenez de la Rueda zipped by them on his Vespa along the Paseo Maritimo," he said. "His wavy black hair, healthy olive-toned complexion, piercing brown eyes and air of vigorous youthfulness gave every indication that he was of Spanish origin."

The Mediterranean island of Mallorca was converted into an expatriate British colony in the 1960s. Since 1984 it has been illegal to be of Spanish descent, unless in possession of a special visa issued by the Consulate for construction workers. Mr Jimenez de la Rueda had not been in possession of any such visa at the time of his arrest.

"He was basically flouting every immigration law in the land," continued Mr Burghley-Wittington. "My officers followed him for a few hours, to see whether they were mistaken, but it was soon clear that this was a bona fide Spaniard. Mr Jimenez de la Rueda picked up his girlfriend from college and they went to have an ice cream. After that he dropped in to say hello to his grandmother and then he had a game of tennis with his uncle. These are not the activities of an Englishman."

"We don't really approve of dark skin," added the Major's wife Lady Henrietta, Duchess of Magaluf. "Suntans are only acceptable with a lobster hue, and they must appear on wrinkled, leathery skin. Mr Jimenez de la Rueda's tan was clearly hereditary,

Juan José Jimenez de la Rueda with his girlfriend Imaculada

and it was quite evident that it extended all the way down to – well, one can only imagine. Probably the buttocks are as smooth and brown as the youthful, radiant visage and the firm, powerful forearms. We don't really allow that sort of thing here," she repeated, taking large draughts from her gin and tonic.

Mr Jimenez de la Rueda will be tried at Palma Magistrates Court next Tuesday.

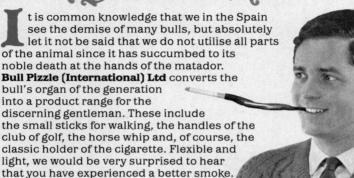

MYHTHS & LEGENDS:
THE LEGEND OF DON ROLFINO

THERE IS A STATUE in a small square in Barcelona commemorating a singular fellow who, according to Catalan legend, arrived on these shores from Italy in the 18th century. This mysterious traveller, who called himself Don Rolfino, would arrive in towns and villages in Spain and install himself in the main square, with his luggage stacked neatly around him. He then proceeded to await his reception from the Mayor or some local dignitary. The reception never came – for nobody in the village or town was expecting Don Rolfino. No wires had been forwarded to precede Rolfino's arrival, no delegates had called to announce his identity or the purpose of his visit. He merely stood attentively in the square, hat in hand, a charming smile fixed on his mouth, with one hand extended as if about to shake someone's hand.

After several sightings in regions of Spain as remote as the Basque Country, La Mancha and Extremadura, the word began to circulate about the mysterious stranger's arrival. When he had installed himself in the main square, small children would run up and shake his outstretched hand; ladies would curtsey at him and men would doff their hats. He would politely acknowledge these gestures yet remain aloof and absorbed, as if looking over their shoulders in expectation of a greeting from someone of higher rank.

Before long, no town in Spain felt complete until it had received a visit from Don Rolfino. It was never known where he would arrive next, since the direction of his peregrinations seemed to bear no logical scrutiny. Nevertheless, villages that hadn't been graced with a visit would make preparations for such an eventuality. Meetings would be held in council chambers, the main square would be cleaned and buildings given a lick of paint. In some cases, new trees were planted in the square and a small marquee was erected. A speech was written by the mayor, the local brass band put in some extra practice, and children were told to expect a day off school, should Don Rolfino ever arrive.

In the end, Don Rolfino was received wherever he went with the fanfare he seemed to have expected from the start. He spent the rest of his life touring Spain, attending lavish receptions and ceremonies to honour his arrival. He was even invited for a second visit to the very places where he had been ignored during his early years, with the promise of a more suitable welcome this time. The statue in Plaza Rolfino, Barcelona, commemorates the first known sighting of Don Rolfino in Spain.

Naples, Italy, 20th November

At last we are becalmed – both emotionally and climatically. It has been a tempestuous week on a number of fronts and it is a great relief that differences have been settled and a level footing has finally been regained. I'm afraid that over the last seven days I have managed to fall out with both Masaki and Gustav over entirely unrelated issues.

My relations with Masaki were sorely tested back in Barcelona due to an unfortunate misunderstanding of a rather embarrassing nature. He accosted me outside our suite in the hotel corridor one morning, and unaccountably started to pull at my trousers in a most alarming manner, insisting in no uncertain terms that I relinquish my underwear. It has always been my opinion that a man's nether regions are very much his own domain, and it was only much later, after I had dealt the poor fellow a couple of robust blows from my cane, that the truth emerged. Gustav had asked him to attend to the laundry and he had merely been attempting to effect his duties.

Unfortunately both Gustav and Masaki were unaware that I had already made ample provision in the underwear department. Prior to leaving Blighty I had made an excursion to Pouves & Peartree (Expeditionary Suppliers) Ltd. and purchased 52 identical pairs of stout heavy-duty hessian undershorts. I was assured by the assistant that they are indispensable wear for the world traveller, sidetracking the need for a laundry as, at the end of the week, each pair is merely thrown away. Nevertheless, despite being apprised of this information, Masaki spent the next five days skulking about me like a wounded cur.

After staying in the Presidential Suite, Gustav and I found it unimaginable that we should embark on the next stretch of the journey in anything other than consummate luxury. Our funds seemed to be haemorrhaging, but we merely turned a blind eye and sent Masaki to search the docks for an ocean-going yacht to hire. Despite his resentments towards me, he certainly did us proud. He returned with news of a handsome 52-footer by the name of The Andromeda. We were going to travel in style.

The owner/skipper, one Miguel Nuñez de Queuvedo, a swarthy fellow with a lazy eye and indescribable halitosis, was very happy to welcome us on board, and on the next tide we set sail from the marina onto a crystal clear sea. Although at first we felt no natural warmth towards Miguel, he proved a splendid raconteur, regaling us with salty tales of piracy, battle and myth. One, which particularly caught Gustav's imagination, was the claim that a colony of sirens had established itself on the stony outcrops of the Strait of Bonifacio (the treacherous rock-strewn channel between Corsica and Sardinia). Sirens for some unfathomable reason have been compelled since the time of Odysseus to lure unsuspecting sea-going folk to their doom by the simple expedient of trilling like demented canaries. Being a modern and rational man, Gustav wanted to put the story to the test, but Miguel only agreed to sail via the Strait with one proviso. Either for effect or out of genuine fear, he insisted that we have our ears sealed with wax to avoid the alluring call of the sirens. He maintained that if Gustav wished to witness the call first hand he must consent to being bound to the mainsail with sturdy rope. As he was dressed in a particularly beautiful houndstooth suit, Gustav was disinclined to consent to treatment that might result in the creasing or misshaping of his sartorial requisites.

By the time we found ourselves adjacent to the imposing cliffs of Bonifacio the sky had turned a charcoal grey and Gustav had been below deck for a good forty minutes. All at once the door of the cabin burst open and there was Gustav, his eyes blazing. I immediately drew the inescapable conclusion that he had been copiously indulging in the contents of our medicine cabinet. "Ah, the sirens, the sirens, they beckon!" he cried, and lunged for the side of the boat. It was all that Miguel and I could do to cling on to his arms as he ranted and raged. "Unhand my immaculate cloth," he bellowed. Despite the undeniable elegance of his attire, we were obliged to bail him unceremoniously into the cabin and lock the door.

Our trials were not yet over, as no sooner had we saved Gustav from certain drowning, a violent squall came drifting in from the east and once we had reached the Tyrrhenian Sea we had to heave to for several hours for fear of being capsized. Gustav was in a fearful bate by the time we sailed into the Gulf of Naples. He has little memory of the incident, but once I related the course of events he accused me of being solely responsible for a deliberate violation of his lapel region and an unsightly tear in his lower gusset.

Thankfully, as I have said all is now tranquil. A fine dinner at the Hotel Vesuvio where we presently reside has put us in much finer spirits, and some jolly expeditions to Pompeii and Herculaneum have spread cordiality amongst us once again.

ART & CULTURE:
MUSEO CRIMINE DI MODO

THE MUSEUM OF Crimes of Fashion in Milan has always been a favourite of mine. The Italians may frequently veer wildly from good taste when it comes to clothes, but on the whole their principled approach to fashion is commendable. And if it occasionally borders on the downright fascist, who is going to argue with them?

The museum is laid out thematically rather than chronologically, with galleries devoted to various aspects of fashion faux pas. These include: inappropriate neckwear (ties with piano keys etc); vulgar waistcoats; trousers with excessive pockets; shirts with lower middle-class detailing (single cuffs, button-down collars etc); overdone nightwear (pyjamas with Hussar facings, dressing gowns with embroidered dragons etc); and an entire gallery demonstrating the shocking effects of incorrect co-ordination. The health warning over this particular gallery is fully justified. I myself nearly had a fainting fit when I witnessed black shoes worn with a tweed suit, even on a dummy, and as for the unholy marriage between tennis shoes and a pin-striped suit – words fail me.

MUSEO CRIMINE DI MODO
Rua Poco Novo 18, Milano 39216
Open Monday-Saturday 10am-6pm
Entry €6

COCKTAILS
HOW TO MIX THEM

THE MILANESE MARTINI

At Giovanni's Bar in Milan, an order for a Dry Martini throws the staff into a frenzy of activity. Firstly, the Maitre d' wheels a small trolley to your table with several bottles of gin and vodka. Once you have selected your spirit, a second waiter comes out with a selection of vermouths. A third waiter then appears with another trolley, bearing a martini glass and a large perfume bottle. With a lot of *eccos* and unctuous smiles, he 'perfumes' the inside of the glass with a couple of sprays of vermouth. Out comes the Maitre d' again with the vodka or gin, which is so chilled that he must wear special gloves to handle the bottle. With a flourish worthy of a priest performing a baptism, he tops up the glass with spirit and wipes the rim with a piece of lemon rind, before backing away with lots of obsequious mutterings.

THE RECIPE:

**10 parts Stolichnaya Cristal Vodka
Fragrance of Vermouth
Sliver of lemon rind**

BY
' ROBERT '

OF THE AMERICAN BAR,
CASINO MUNICIPAL, NICE,
AND LATE OF THE
EMBASSY CLUB, LONDON

ART & CULTURE:
THE HOLY COIFFURE OF SAN GABBRIELE DI BARNETTI

HOUSED IN THE CHURCH of Santa Lucia fiori le Mura on the Via Conte Verde, Rome, the reliquary of the 18th century Capuchin monk, Fra Gabbriele di Barnetti has become one of the major destinations for Italian pilgrims since his canonisation in 1967.

During his lifetime Fra Gabriele was renowned for the consummate beauty of his hair-do. From an early age he had honed his coiffure as an act of "self-beatification for the greater glory of God", but this unconventional theology eventually brought him in conflict with the church hierarchy. In 1771 he was prosecuted for heresy by Pope Clement XIV. During the trial he was accused of flouncing about in an unseemly manner and putting personal vanity before service to God, but in a speech of self-justification that lasted over four and a half hours he managed to convince his accusers that his daily grooming rituals were in actual fact highly potent "prayers in action".

After the dismissal of the case, "touching the coiffure of Fra Gabriele" soon became regarded as a miraculous cure for a variety of ailments (including alopecia, acne and congenital ugliness). So much so that after his death his scalp was removed and displayed in a specially built side chapel in the Church of Santa Lucia.

In commemorative services held four times a year (on Sept. 28th, Dec. 18th, March 11th

and June 15th) pilgrims are granted the right to touch the holy relic. The tarnished receptacle in which the relic is kept is processed around the church and presented to those deemed most deserving of its curative powers. Many miracles have been reported over the years, but from anecdotal evidence it seems that what impresses the visitor most is that the five inch side parting and brilliotined lustre have remained mysteriously uncorrupted by time, and the hair style seems as current and stylish now as when it was detached from San Gabriele's sacred cranium in 1794.

Philpott's
Diseases, Infirmities and Afflictions for the Travelling Connoisseur   98

St. Vitus' Elbow
(External humeral epicodysanvitus)

This disease of the central nervous system is highly prevalent in Italy, and causes the muscles of the upper arm and forearm to contract involuntarily whilst the patient is speaking. This has the effect of sending the elbow joint into convulsions, resulting in excessive gesticulation. Although most doctors believe that the condition is not contagious, it does seem to effect those who spend any lengthy time in Italy, leading to the conclusion that environmental factors must play a significant part in the condition. In the latter stages, involuntary verbal outbursts may also be observed, combined with a tendency to fly into a theatrical rage and argue about even the most innocuous minor irritations. Unfortunately there is no known cure, but if the patient leaves the country before the condition becomes too advanced, there can be some alleviation of the symptoms.

Fig 124. Advanced tertiary case.

Zagreb, Croatia, 28th November

I write this from the rather unsalubrious surroundings
of the Hotel Prvinica, Zagreb. The sleeping form of
Victor rattles noisily a few inches from the only table
in the room. A further few inches away from him is
Masaki, sleeping the sleep of the just. I don't think he
quite understood what he was getting himself into when
taking on this voyage, since in the last few days his
role has broadened somewhat from that of adjudicator.

The trouble began in Naples. We had agreed upon hiring
a car for the next leg of the journey, since we were
connected to Zagreb by some formidable Roman roads. We
dispatched Masaki to search for a suitable vehicle,
furnishing him with a large stack of Euros. He returned
a few hours later with a nasty old Fiat with dents in
the bonnet and scratches all over the sides.

"You blithering idiot, this isn't a hire car," I told
him. "Hire cars are red, shiny things with stereo
systems and air conditioning."

A flicker of exasperation hovered over Masaki's
features for precisely half a second. "Italian car very
expensive to rent, but cheap to buy. After one journey,
we throw away."

I had to admit that the inscrutable one had a point. Once we reached Zagreb the car would be useless to us, since we would have to find a different form of transport for the next leg of the journey.

Rural Italy is really rather charming when viewed from the inside of a car. Shades of burnt umber, vermillion, terracotta and yellow ochre flit past, as if Canaletto or Titian were daubing them directly on to the windscreen. As we penetrated into Browning's "wind aggrieved Appenines", I began to notice a distinct rattle emanating from behind the back seat of the car. Masaki pulled over and I sauntered out to inspect the boot.

Horror of horrors! Curled up inside the boot there was a lady! Alive, though bound hand and foot with stout twine and clearly in great distress. We hauled her out and loosened her shackles and her gag, upon which a torrent of incomprehensible oaths issued forth. As soon as her hands (which I must say were as exquisitely appointed as the rest of her) were untied, communication became relatively easy. Gabriella, as she was named, explained that she was the daughter of a wealthy Tuscan who owed money to some unsavoury Sicilians. Masaki, it seems, had purchased our vehicle from some other ne'er-do-well, who probably saw a golden opportunity when the two villians' backs were turned. We had heard things like this about the Neapolitans.

Gabriella begged to come with us into Yugoslavia, where she would be safer. Neither myself nor Victor had any objection to this - she was, after all, rather a fetching little creature, if a tad noisy for my taste. I asked her if she had a passport with her, and it was clear from her downcast expression that she didn't. "Then one of us will have to marry her. I suggest we draw cocktail sticks."

Masaki drew the longest stick, and as soon as we arrived in Trieste, we located the registry office. They must have thought they'd seen it all, until Masaki took his wedding vows with all the emotion of someone trying on a pair of trousers in Marks & Spencer. Victor and I left the young lovebirds to enjoy their first evening together, while we went in search of Trieste's finest Dry Martini.

When we returned, there was quite a commotion outside our hotel. A man was standing in the shadows under a balcony, while items of hotel furniture were being hurled at him from above. We thought perhaps a pop group had rolled into town, until I noticed the unmistakably stoical, upright, expressionless visage of Masaki on the figure under the awning. I looked up to see Gabriella, hands raised above her head, a stream of oaths issuing from her throat.

"What the devil's afoot, Masaki?" I cried, dodging out of the way of a flying television set.

"Master need to explain to lady about duties of English manservant," he stated in his enigmatic manner. It turned out that old Gabriella had taken this whole marriage lark a little too seriously, and expected Masaki to fulfil his nuptial duties in the boudoir. I hastened upstairs, and explained to Gabriella that Masaki was a gentleman's gentleman with impeccable credentials, and as such inhabited a plane of existence prohibitive of acts of conjugal unpleasantness. This produced another stream of choice language, and some hand signals which seriously questioned the fecundity of the British male. I promised Gabriella that we'd arrange a divorce as soon as we reached Zagreb.

After only two weeks on the road, poor Masaki has now experienced far more than he probably ever expected to in a lifetime. Yet to us he is beginning to prove indispensable; his po-faced manner seems to strike fear into European officials. The magistrate in Zagreb who dealt with the divorce today was very unhelpful to start with, wittering on about documents and seals and bureaucracy, but as soon as he saw Masaki looming over his desk, the process suddenly went very smoothly.

Croatia Today

Edition No.: 1,724 / 28th November   CROATIA'S PREMIER DAILY ENGLISH LANGUAGE NEWSPAPER

ORGANISED CRIME IN 'STYLE WAKE-UP CALL'

Croatia's recent efforts to seek closer economic ties with its westerly neighbours and its aspiration to full EU membership have had some unusual and unexpected knock-on effects within the country's extensive criminal underworld.

Radovan Furjanic surveys samples from his extensive bun running operation.

After the break up of Yugoslavia it was sadly no surprise that a period of lawlessness and instability ensued, but now one of Croatia's mafia dons seems to be growing tired of the traditional vulgar predictabilities of dealing in illicit firearms, prostitution and designer drugs, and wishes to cut more of a dash with the upper echelons of Croatian society. He has therefore circulated a memo, which he refers to as his "style wake-up call" to his henchmen and rival mafia chiefs outlining a new code of ethics and range of activities that he believes will enable the criminal underground to maintain the kudos of their bad-boy credentials whilst embracing the English gentleman's standards of elegant refinement.

Some old habits die hard and Radovan Furjanic cannot quite bring himself to abandon his dealing in illicit drugs, but his memo does express the intention to "move our interests away from kiddies' drugs such as ecstacy, cocaine and heroine, and to concentrate

our efforts on the drugs of choice of the mature English fop such as laudanum and morphine".

He goes on to outline some new arenas of gangland activity. "Our Firm now has the intention of starting our country's largest Bun Running operation bringing large quantities of eccles cakes, hot cross buns and toasted tea cakes into every corner of the land. This is an area where we believe that huge profits are waiting to be made."

And he has no intention of stopping there, further areas include extensive shirt laundering activities and hefty investment into what he calls the White Knave Trade.

"In today's Croatia many of the top families have a love affair with the English cad, such as your Terry-Thomas. We lure good-for-nothing sons of posh families in the UK out to Croatia with the promise of free acting residency, we then show them a lot of Terry-Thomas videos and finally sell them on to wealthy Croatian families as their pet cad or bounder. Even if they are initially a bit too nice a few months of captivity soon makes them pretty mean. In the end, they steal, they lie, they throw wine over guests' trousers. Ha ha ha! He he he!" he explains.

■ Story continues on page 4, 5 & 6.

President Stjepan Mesi   HOSTAL PRVINICA, ZAGREB
Presidential Palace
Zagreb, Yugoslavia

28th November

Most esteemed Sir,

Following a wager with some chums at London's Sheridan Club, I am travelling in the
company of Mr Vic Darkwood and our manservant, Mr Masaki Nakatake. Due to an
unfortunate incident in Italy involving some Mafiosi ruffians, we took it upon
ourselves to save a young lady from a rather nasty scrape by allowing her to wed Mr
Nakatake. Through no-one's fault in particular, this marriage is a farce and both
parties desire to have it terminated immediately.
     May I remind you of the kindness bestowed upon your nation in 1944 by the great
Winston Churchill? As you know, your King Peter II and his pregnant wife had taken
refuge in Claridges, London, having fled from the Nazi invasion of Belgrade. In order
for their son to inherit the throne, he had to be born on Yugoslav soil, so Churchill
arranged for suite 212 of Claridges to become Yugoslav territory for the day. This
small gesture of diplomacy resulted in the reinstatement, 54 years later, of Prince
Alexander in the Royal Palace of Belgrade.
     I was wondering whether, as a return favour, you would consider making room 4 of the
Hostal Prvinica into British territory for the day? This would give the British Consul
temporary jurisdiction to effect a divorce between our two reluctant spouses. Your
help in this matter would be greatly appreciated, and upon my return to Blighty I
shall inform Mr Anthony Blair that you are 'owed one' by the British government.

I have the honour to remain,
Your humble and admiring servant,

Gustav Temple

PRESIDENTIAL PALACE, ZAGREB, CROATIA

30th November

Dear Mr Temple,

As you may or may not know, the former Yugoslavia has gone through some changes
since Mr Churchill's generous gesture in 1944. One of these is the partitioning of the
country into four smaller countries, not all of whom share common goals. Prince
Alexander's ambition is to become king of Serbia-Montenegro, while our plans for the
future here in Croatia do not involve him in the slightest.
     I respectfully suggest that you try your luck with the President of Serbia-Montenegro.
In the meantime, I enclose a copy of "The Former Yugoslavia – Where Now?" which I
hope you will find useful and informative.

Yours sincerely,

Stjepan Mesi
President
Croatia (*not* Yugoslavia)

BODY ODDIFICATION

The Terry-Thomas

THE COMEDIC MOVIE actor Mr Norman Wisdom is rumoured to have acquired the status of a deity with the film-going public of Albania, but in Croatia, it is Mr Terry-Thomas who attracts the adulation. A natural and wholesome admiration for this screen cad has led many impressionable young fans to attempt to emulate the star's instantly recognisable and irregular dentation. This is generally achieved by slowly driving the front teeth apart through the introduction of a gradually increased quantity of cocktail sticks during the hours of sleep.

TRUBSHAWE'S
Oddification Rating
★ ☆ ☆ ☆

ART & CULTURE:

MUSEUM OF MOUSTACHES

A JOURNEY THROUGH Eastern Europe is simply not complete without a visit to the Museum of Moustaches in Budapest. Hungary ranks with Belgium as one of the great moustache-growing regions of the world. Visitors to the capital will rarely glimpse a naked upper lip on a male over the age of fifteen, and locally produced moustache wax Zwirbel-Paste enjoys a worldwide reputation for excellence.

The museum itself contains every form of moustache found in every corner of the globe, from the sleazy Mexican Zapata style to the Hapsburg Empire pomposity of what is known simply as "The Hungarian" (pictured).

Also on display is a collection of unusual moustache paraphernalia such as snoods, miniature combs, soup protectors and the coloured beads worn in moustaches by the Arambi people of eastern Patagonia.

Thessaloniki, Greece, 2nd December

So here we are at last in Thessaloniki. We have booked into the thoroughly charming Egnatia Hotel and we are settling down for a well-deserved session with the briar. Personally I am a trifle fearful that we find ourselves on the cusp of leaving the relative certainties of Europe and entering the wilder realms that lie beyond. Luckily we have a couple of days to gather our pluck before the onward march, giving us a little time for seeing the sights in this ancient city.

After the matrimonial shenanigans of last week and our final happy extrication from that raucous harpy, peace and quiet reigned over our little band once more. Although Gustav and I had been initially seduced by Gabriella's svelte packaging, the horror of discovering that the woman possessed very little by way of volume control had set our nerves on edge and made our final release from her the cause of some celebration. Thus it was (coupled with other circumstances that will presently become apparent) that I spent the major part of the journey from Zagreb in the state of profound inebriation.

Before I surrendered my soul to Madame Alcohol's tender embrace, however, there were important decisions to be made. With a bit of foresight we had realised that we would be ill advised to use up all luxurious modes of transport in the first half of our around-the-world peregrinations. If we did, we knew we would be compelled in the final stages to succumb to the ignominies of ox cart, lawn mower or pogo stick. With this in mind we decided against our better judgement that on the next leg of the tour we should consider "roughing it" a little. In 'roughing it' we had no intention of revisiting the abject misery of the pony and cart. No, indeed, when a fellow lowers his standards he should always endeavour to lower them in style. We knew by now that we could trust Masaki's intuition in this matter and dispatched him at once to track down a suitable form of conveyance.

Two hours later Masaki returned astride a most impressive beast. Apparently to aficionados the Triumph Bonneville T140E is a king amongst motorbikes and the fact that it was provided with a capacious sidecar delighted us beyond measure. It was only after a few hours of cogitation that we realised that things weren't as rosy as we had thought. The bike might be adequate to accommodate three people, but there was the little matter of luggage to consider. We contemplated various configurations, but in the end understood that the only practicable arrangement would be if Gustav and I travelled on the bike whilst Masaki and the luggage were stowed in the sidecar. Even so we were faced with the need to jettison at least half of our luggage in order to get on board.

Words cannot convey the wailing and misery that ensued. Gustav wept openly as he was forced relinquish three quarters of his wardrobe. Tenderly he stroked each trouser leg of his flannels as Masaki prised them from his fingers.

"Bear up, old stick," I averred, barely being able to disguise the tremolo in my voice, "we can have the whole lot forwarded by train to St Petersburg, and meet up with them later."

Gustav indignantly pulled himself up to full height. "You don't understand, there are standards to be maintained. Are you seriously suggesting that I should spend the next 3000 miles in a state of sartorial inadequacy? It's all right for you with that suit of yours."

Gustav was referring to my ancestral suit, a garment that had done three generations of Darkwood proud, and although it had taken a terrible battering over the last few weeks was still going strong.

"We all have to make sacrifices. How do you suppose I will be able to endure life without these?" At this point, I am ashamed to say I too broke down and sobbed uncontrollably. At my feet, there lay some of my most treasured requisites. A crate of Thedgleley's Chunky-Cut "Olde Tyme" Marmalade, an exquisitely tooled fold-away travel cocktail bar and three large leather trunks containing a wide range of single malts, vintage wines and ports (including two bottles of Barros Colheita 1950).

"No! No, we can't leave the cocktail bar," muttered Gustav in a tone of disbelief. I had to concede he was right. Now, that would have been going too far.

As we had 24 hours before the off, I set about making decisions about what to take and what to forward. I swiftly came to the conclusion that if I could not take all of the trunks and bottles with me, that did not preclude me from taking some of their contents. I therefore set about decanting two bottles of Islay single malt, one of the Barros Colheitas and a delightful Chateau Beychevelle, St. Julien 1959 into the lower recesses of my digestive system.

I have no recollection of the journey that followed, but now in Thessoloniki I am aching from head to toe after having sustained numerous cuts and abrasions. Gustav has informed me that I only fell off the back of bike four times along the way. I dare say it was my relaxed state that saved me from injuries of a more serious nature.

MYTHS & LEGENDS:
POLYESTA AND LINENUS

ONE OF THE MOST charming of the Greek myths is that of the rivalry between the evil giant Polyesta, and the refined Linenus. Linenus, together with his brothers, Poplines and Cottonaeus, were the sole manufacturers of the cloth of the Gods. Polyesta was consumed with envy and conspired with Vulcan to invent a new cloth that would usurp Linenus's monopolisation of the toga market. Linenus and Polyesta were both asked to present their sales pitches to Zeus on the top of Mount Olympus. Zeus was so impressed by the sparks of electricity emitted by Polyesta's cloth, he decided to try on one of his garments, but soon discovered that the toga was irritatingly clingy and made him sweat in a most unseemly manner. Polyesta was thus banished into the lower depths of Hades, leaving Linenus to corner the market for the rest of history.

GRECIAN TIMES

4TH JUNE. MORNING EDITION 16,230. INCORPORATING THE AEGEAN CHRONICLE & MESSENGER

First Lady of Athos

OURANOUPOLIS, 4TH JUNE

Helena Theodopolus has become the first lady ever to set foot on Mount Athos.

The community of Byzantine monasteries has prohibited the entry of women since an edict by Emperor Constantine issued in AD 1060. Ms Theodopolus managed to gain entry to the peninsula, which is open to visits by male pilgrims, by dressing as a man. Apart from simply proving that it could be done, Ms Theodopolus wanted to make a statement against Greek attitudes towards women. Ms Theodopolus is certainly in a position to comment on issues regarding femininity.

When I interviewed her she was wearing a fetching blouse that displayed a generous view of her décolletage, her lovely legs were showed off by a tiny little mini skirt, and she had a habit of tossing her luxuriant blonde hair about while she explained the political motivation for her assault on Athos. "It is high time that the Greek government realised that women have got a voice as well as a body," she said, brushing a strand of blonde hair out of her eyes. "This country's record on women's rights is deplorable."

Ms Theodopolus explained how she planned the assault. "Well, as you can

imagine it was not easy to disguise such a feminine body as a man! I had to use heavy strips of cloth to bind my breasts. But disguising my make-up was the most difficult part. I used a combination of fake tan and a strategically placed wide-brimmed fedora. I managed to lower my voice a few octaves by smoking a pipe for several weeks and having a glass of cognac for breakfast."

Ms Theodopolus took the boat from Ouranoupolis with other pilgrims. She had slight difficulty disembarking at Athos, and was almost rumbled when she put out a petite hand with varnished nails to be steadied. But the Greek boatman took her for a homosexual and laughingly helped her ashore, giving her a pat on the bottom for good measure. Once inside the monastic community, Ms Theodopolus was able to roam freely around the

various buildings open to the public. Her first view of the monasteries did not provide a favourable impression.

"There was dust everywhere," she says, "and the windows clearly hadn't been cleaned for centuries. I wasn't allowed into the monks' dormitories, of course, but the basketfuls of dirty habits outside them told the whole story." Was there anything positive in what she saw in an all-male society? She thought for a moment, before her pretty face lit up. "Yes, yes! Guess what I saw? A lovely little kitten! I gave it one of my chocolates and played with it, until one of the monks started giving me funny looks, and I thought I might have given the game away. All the other men were just ignoring this cutesy little kitten!" I reminded her that female cats are the only female species allowed on Athos, presumably to keep the rat population down.

So in terms of Ms Theodopolus's political statement, did she feel she had made her point by being the first female to enter Mount Athos? "I hope the Greek government will finally sit up and listen to women, now that I have shown them that we do really have a voice." Ms Theodopolus took her leave, but not before showing me her crocodile skin handbag. "I didn't see many of these on Mount Athos!" she laughed.

Victor Agamemnon Darkwood Esq.
Suite 17, The Sheridan Club, St. James's, London SW1

Evangelos Venizelos
Greek Minister of Culture
20-22 Bouboulinas Str., 106 82 Athens

EGNATIA HOTEL, Antigonidon Str.16
Thessaloniki, Greece 54630
Evangelos Venizelos

Dear Sir,

As an Englishman staying in your charming city of Thessaloniki I am moved to write to you to express how struck I have been by the huge wealth of archaeological heritage that your country has to offer.

In a recent discussion with my travel companion, Mr Temple, regarding the on-going debate about the Parthenon Marbles (which you may recall were saved for posterity by Lord Elgin in 1799) we found ourselves in whole-hearted agreement with the concerns of the Greek Government. We concur without quibble that seeing the so-called "Elgin" marbles out of the context of their natural home of the Parthenon, which they originally decorated, makes a mockery of art history. Fortunately, Gustav and I have come up with an elegant solution to this thorny dilemma.

With your agreement, we propose to have the Parthenon carefully demolished, each stone numbered and the entire building shipped to London. It is our understanding that the levels of pollution in Athens are detrimental to historical artefacts and the fact that there are a number of other buildings on the Acropolis hill will probably mean that it will not be greatly missed.

Naturally we wouldn't expect you to incur any of the costs involved in the dismantling of the monument. I have a very good contact in the building trade, Reg Higgins from Dollis Hill, who comes highly recommended by Gustav. Apparently Mr Higgins did a marvellous job installing a fountain of Bacchus in his back garden and tiling his bathroom. Everyone who has visited the latter says that Mr Higgins' grouting has to be seen to be believed. I feel confident that when the British Government learn of his "very competitive rates" they will wish to use no other contractor.

We are staying in Thessaloniki for only one more night so please feel free to use the enclosed carrier pigeon for reply purposes.

Cordial regards

Victor Darkwood

EVANGELOS VENIZELOS
MINISTER OF CULTURE
HELLENIC MINISTRY OF CULTURE, 20-22 BOUBOULINAS STR., 106 82 ATHENS

4th December

Dear Mr Darkwood,

Mr. Venizelos apologises that he is unable to reply to your letter personally, but has asked me to thank you for your novel solution to a problem that has been dogging the Greek Government for many years.

HELIOS ACIDOPHILUS
Personal Private Secretary to the Minister of Culture

PS. Mr. Venizelos also wonders whether you could let him have Mr. Higgins' phone number as he is considering having a new fitted kitchen installed in his Athens apartment.

Asia

Istanbul, Turkey, 9th December

We are now installed comfortably in the faded splendour
of the Pera Palace Hotel, Istanbul. An ancient
chandelier, seemingly held together by cobwebs, dangles
precariously over a dusty old chaise longue, upon which
Victor is sprawled, exuding plumes of pungent navy shag
from his meerschaum. Masaki looms in and out of the room
wearing a ludicrous white face mask to protect him from
the dust. For the first time on this mammoth voyage,
Victor and myself feel vaguely at home. I had a feeling
that as soon as we penetrated Byzantium we would feel
closer to what we loosely term our God.

Thessaloniki was pleasant enough, if a little middle
European for my taste. I had been hoping for a glimpse of
the Ottoman glories that were to come, but the Turks had
left few reminders of their 500-year occupation of the
city. Victor had insisted on searching for some obscure
little brothel which Brian Sewell had stayed in once,
endlessly repeating a line he had read in that peculiar
author's *South From Ephesus* about "sear and yellow leaves
of passion". Victor seemed genuinely intent on locating
the very shower tray in which Mr Sewell had observed
these used prophylactics. My travelling companion's idea
of "seeing the sights" is beginning to concern me.

There was not much else to detain us in Thessaloniki.
Masaki, having made a few discreet inquiries, ascertained
that an equine transfer to Istanbul would be most
appropriate, the journey not exceeding some 400 miles.
There seemed something heroic, nay Byronic, about riding
into Constantinople on horseback, and I made a mental
note to purchase a turban the minute we set foot there.

My only experience of horses, though extensive, has been
to watch them jumping over hurdles ridden by somebody
else, usually with a large wad of cash riding on the

outcome. I have never given more thought to the jockey than to assume he is a little Irish fellow who pilots the nag as efficaciously as possible. My first attempts to leave Thessaloniki convinced me to pay more respect to these fellows. The nags Masaki had purchased had clearly been trained for dressage rather than transportation, for they spent the best part of the morning cavorting around the hotel courtyard and generally kicking up a fuss as soon as we mounted them.

Masaki, of course, took to riding like a fish to water, a fact we attributed to the vestiges of Samurai warrior in him. In the end, the only way we could make a start on our journey was to tie the other two horses to Masaki's mare and leave Thessaloniki as a sort of equine caravan. Not so much the three wise men as two idiotic buffoons and one sage Oriental.

Having spent most of my life with the firm conviction that civilisation ends at the outer edges of London's SW1 postcode, it was only when we entered Istanbul that I began to question this ostensibly logical presumption. The petty bourgeois vulgarity of central Europe, with its gaudy Catholic cathedrals, its repetitive ionic colonnades and the tedious "café society" everyone in England makes such a fuss about; all these things faded into an insignificant distance when we entered the portals of Byzantium. Here was something genuinely worth the effort of travel, a place abounding with mystique, colourful squalor and the promise of hidden depravity. From the golden domes hovering in the orange smog over the city, to the labyrinth of foul-smelling alleys that composed its inner core, I knew that in Constantinople I was entering my Elysium, my Arcadia, my Xanadu.

The Turkish youth were very taken with us, crowding around our steeds and hopping about as if the Shah of Persia had just rolled into town. Straining to make out their broken English, it seemed they were all offering us some welcoming gift - belly dancers, carpets, hasheesh, baubles and trinkets. We thanked them profusely and asked to be led to the Pera Palace, the hotel considered de rigueur among the Grand Tourists of the 19th century. While Masaki booked us into a suite, I took the opportunity to mingle with the locals, by asking some of the charming fellows who had followed us there where our horses might be stabled and groomed.

Victor was presented with a ceremonial dagger by a jovial little chap in a fez. He took it to be a gift and inserted it between his braces, but the Turk then requested an extortionate fee. We had not yet sent Masaki to change any money, so I offered the man a shiny tenpence piece.

That was when things turned a little nasty. We suddenly found ourselves surrounded by Turks, all looking rather menacing and demanding money from us for the items we had accepted as gifts. "Look here old thing, there's really no need for all this hullabaloo," said Victor to one of them. "We are Englishmen and we come in peace."

"Ah, Eengerlish!" said one of the Turks. "Manchester United?" From the bag he was carrying he produced a red T-shirt covered in advertising slogans and proffered it to Victor. "You buy Manchester United shirt, yes?"

Victor rubbed the cloth of the T-shirt between his fingers. "No thanks, old man. I wouldn't wear this within fifty yards of a naked flame. Synthetic fibres aren't the thing for a pipe smoker, you know." In the meantime, a pile of items was gathering around us that I think we were expected to purchase. Fingers were being rubbed by one and all in rather an aggressive fashion, and I couldn't see a way out of this most inconvenient situation.

"How much for a boy?" came a voice over my shoulder. The crowd of street vendors parted, to reveal Masaki, making his ludicrous request with his usual po-faced equanimity. "I wish to purchase a small boy for use as a slave," he repeated, to the evident astonishment of the Turks. They gathered about each other and discussed the request, clearly coming to the conclusion that none of them could fulfil it. As if by magic, all the vendors disappeared, and we were left to congratulate Masaki, once again, on his astounding capacity to baffle impertinent foreigners.

ART & CULTURE:
MUSEUM OF HUMILIATING HEADWEAR

ANYONE WITH A MOD-ICUM of interest in the cephalogical history of Turkey should not begrudge themselves a visit to the Istanbul Museum of Humiliating Headwear. When Atatürk banned the fez in 1925, to distance Turkey from its Ottoman past, the new legislation was brought in so hurriedly that Turks had little time to adjust. Islamic rule did not permit them to go about hatless, so milliners in Europe suddenly received unprecedented orders for trilbies, bowlers, Homburgs, Fedoras and panamas. Articles appeared in newspapers on how to wear hats, and even the Istanbul dandies, used to wearing their fezzes at precise, jaunty angles, had difficulty incorporating the new headwear into their pristine wardrobes.

The Istanbul Museum of Humiliating Headwear chronicles this dark era of the transition from fez to western hat. In the glass vitrines one can see crudely fashioned fedoras made from dyed, dissembled fezzes, pink feathered hats with ribbons and flat caps from Yorkshire. Most humiliating of all, in this often distressing museum, is the broad-brimmed Catholic bishop's hat, which made one obedient old man a laughing stock in Sinop when he first wore it after the ban had been imposed. He was so incensed that he took his hat to the governor's office, stamped up and down on it and offered himself up for arrest.

MUSEUM OF HUMILIATING HEADWEAR
Ziyad Street 24,
Istanbul 34157
Open Mon-Fri 10am-6pm
Entry Free

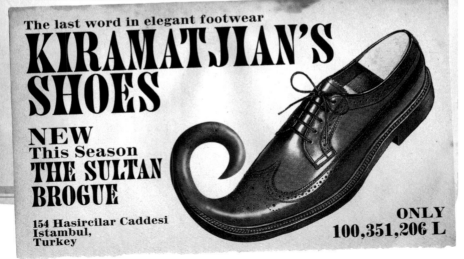

ODETTE L'ODALISQUE
A REAL TURKISH DELIGHT

**ODETTE SINGS! ODETTE DANCES!
ODETTE'S FRIENDS COME ROUND!
ODETTE TAKES A BATH!**
(AND YOU CAN TOO)

**HAREM OPENING HOURS 5-11PM
ALL MAJOR CREDIT CARDS ACCEPTED
0428 92 93 67**

TURKISH TIMES

No. 1,237 Price: 1,500,000 L

December 12th

"SMOKING SAVED MY LIFE" CLAIMS EARTHQUAKE VICTIM

AN ASTOUNDING STORY of endurance and resourcefulness emerged this week after an earthquake victim attributed his 21 days of survival beneath the rubble of his demolished home to his habit of smoking a hasheesh pipe.

Yusuf Ozal, a 37-year-old metal worker from Central Anatolia, has claimed that his pipe, a traditional Arabian hookah, provided him with all the equipment he needed to remain alive throughout his ordeal.

"I was reclining on my divan in a very relaxed state when the earthquake started," recalls Yusuf. "At first I found it amusing, I just laughed, but then the ground really started shaking and various pots and pans began to fall from the shelves. Shortly after that the whole ceiling caved in on me."

When Mr Ozal regained consciousness he realised he had been buried alive. "I frantically felt about me to try to gauge where I was and then in the pitch black I stumbled upon my trusty hookah," he says.

Don't bogart that hookah. Mr Ozal takes a toke.

For the next three weeks Mr Ozal utilised every part of his pipe to make sure he did not perish. He used the water from the bottom of the pipe (traditionally required for cooling tobacco and hasheesh smoke) as an essential reservoir, thus preserving him from dehydration. He removed the nozzle from the hookah and used it as a handy

probe, finally managing to poke it through the accumulated rubble to make a vital breathing hole. He then was able to whistle through the tube in order to attract attention.

"I never gave up hope," he says. "Whenever I started to lose my nerve, I would chew on a prime piece of hasheesh which calmed me down considerably and enabled me to get a few hours' sleep."

He was finally discovered by members of the Sivas fire brigade who were led to Yusuf by the melodious whistling from his pipe nozzle.

"Mr Ozal is a very, very lucky man" says Chief Fire Officer Kasim Hassan. "If it hadn't been for his pronounced fondness for drugs he could well have been a gonner."

"There is a moral in this," muses Mr Ozal. "The world health organisation is always telling us that smoking and drugs are bad for us. I think I should present my experiences to them and then possibly they will have to think again."

St Petersburg, Russia, 16th December

With the benefit of hindsight, it seems that my misgivings about 'beyond Europe' were a trifle premature. Istanbul to St. Petersburg has been easily the most pleasant leg of our journey so far.

I write this in the Room of Ancient Sculpture at the Hermitage Museum sitting across from a very fine 4th century marble of Dionysus with Persephone. Ah, a perfect fusion of art, wine and fecundity – a mirror image of my own dear self, perhaps? Having said that, I have a growing suspicion that my hessian undershorts may shortly put pay to the last of the three – they are beginning to chafe quite horribly.

Although it is past four in the afternoon, Gustav has remained in the hotel with Masaki. He is so delighted at being reunited with our forwarded luggage that he has set about having everything laundered, pressed, and polished to perfection, and has spent hours parading before the full-length looking glass throwing bon mots at his reflection and reciting vast tracts from Baudelaire's Fleurs du Mal.

Back in Istanbul, the hardships of our recent encounters with motorcycle and horse had once again fired within us an insatiable lust for luxury travel. Whilst spending a pleasant afternoon in an antechamber of the hammam, idly smoking the hookah, I had made the acquaintance of one of the locals, a charming fellow (although admittedly with teeth that were in a shocking state of repair) by the name of Shâhrukh. He assured me that he could provide "commodious and delightful" passage to St. Petersburg. Rather too trustingly I handed over a large chunk of lucre. Quite frankly I was pleased to get rid of it. With the exchange rate as it was, the unsightly wads we were being forced to carry were beginning to bag out our pockets and Gustav was starting to worry that the carefully tailored line of his Anderson & Sheppard chalk-stripe would be lost forever.

At the appointed hour Shâhrukh picked us up from the quayside not far from the Bazaar. To our abject horror our 'commodious and delightful' transport turned out to be nothing other than a ramshackle old pantechnicon. On peering into the dimly lit interior we could just make out piles of carpets and furniture, and then, lo and behold, the faint glint of eyes looking back at us. These, it transpired, were some of Shâhrukh's so-called "business associates", or, rather, itinerant black marketeers assisting Shâhrukh in his nefarious dealings backwards and forwards across the Russian border. I have to admit, the idea of sharing our transport for the next 3000 miles with a vanload of cut-throats and brigands had little appeal.

I heard a voice at my shoulder. "The wise man does not leap like the impetuous salmon, Mr Wictor." It was Masaki with some inscrutable nonsense or other. I thought I saw a slight smirk play across the impudent rascal's lips. "No matter, I get to work. It take 20 minutes maximum," he continued.

In a trice Masaki was a whirlwind of action. Flitting hither and thither, disappearing off down nearby alleyways and returning bearing potted plants, hookahs and tea urns; rearranging the furniture in the back of the van and installing our fold-away travel cocktail bar; using some of the rugs as wall-hangings and converting others into sumptuous areas for reclining. By the time he had finished (in precisely 19 minutes and 12 seconds) he had converted the pantechnicon into the most opulent interior imaginable. The occupants of the van, on reappraisal, turned out to be a pretty cheery bunch too and to our great delight nearly all possessed talents which would seem incongruous with their chosen careers of peddling contraband. One was an accomplished player of the baglama (a curious sort of lute instrument); another, a lady, swathed herself in chiffon and sequins and exhibited an unexpected talent for contortionism and cavorting about in the most shameless of manners; and yet another was an amusing dwarf who was more than willing to act as an impromptu waiter handing round the canapés. How we smoked. How we sang. How we laughed.

To avoid highwaymen and kidnappers that are rumoured to loiter in the vicinity of the Ukraine we took the circuitous route around the southern shore of the Black Sea. For seven days we travelled, stopping off at caravanserais and lay-bys along the way and throughout the journey the festivities did not abate. We must have made an odd spectacle when we arrived on Nevskiy Prospekt, St. Petersburg at 2 in the morning, stumbled out of the back of the pantechnicon accompanied by billowing hasheesh fumes and dressed in turbans, loose fitting robes and exotic embroidered slippers. The trip had been exhilarating.

Now we are resident at the Winter Garden Hotel and tremendously looking forward to a little exploration, a little caviar and a little vodka. Before we leave Gustav and I are keen to visit Peter the Great's wooden cabin, apparently the first residence built in St. Petersburg in 1703. Although the fellow was a little too aspirational and hearty for our liking, his frequent debaucheries, his encouragement of smoking and his introduction of a beard tax endear us to him. The cabin contains many of the possessions of Tsar Peter and Gustav is particularly curious to observe the precise cut and crease of the great man's trousers.

BODY ODDIFICATION

Cufflink Piercings

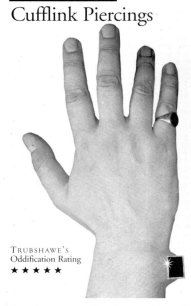

TRUBSHAWE'S
Oddification Rating
★ ★ ★ ★ ★

A MAN BORN to discretion would usually blanch at the thought of having studs, rings and other ironmongery stapled through his nose, eyebrow or lip, but a piercing skewered through the soft flesh on the underside of the wrist is an entirely different matter.

In Russia today, this subtle and convenient placing of body ornamentation is a la mode in all polite circles, enabling fellows of taste and distinction to sport favourite items from their Fabergé cufflink collections even whilst in bed, the bath, or paying a visit to the local sauna.

COCKTAILS
HOW TO MIX THEM

THE MOSCOW MARTINI

I n the days of Khrushchev-era communism in the Soviet Union, supplies of practically every existing comestible were in alarmingly short supply. The exception was vodka, which sometimes filled not just whole aisles, but entire supermarkets. Sergei Ivanov, owner of Sergei's bar in Moscow, was rumoured to possess the city's only bottle of Vermouth. The more sophisticated of Moscow's alcoholics would converge on Sergei's in search of a Dry Martini. Sergei would fill a cocktail glass with premium-quality vodka, then make his way towards the cellar to get the Vermouth. But the endless rows of bottles of vodka ranged along the bar and down the stairway would prove too much of a temptation. Despite many valiant attempts, Sergei never managed to find the bottle of Vermouth, but a lot of fun was had in the process!

THE RECIPE:

**64 parts Russian Vodka
1 part Vermouth (if found)**

BY
'ROBERT'
OF THE AMERICAN BAR,
CASINO MUNICIPAL, NICE,
AND LATE OF THE
EMBASSY CLUB, LONDON

LONELY AND LOOKING FOR LOVE?

YOU TOO CAN FIND THAT SPECIAL SOMEONE WITH

ENGLISH HOUSE HUSBANDS

Tired of being alone? If you are seriously looking for love then why not let us introduce you to one of our gorgeous English House Husbands. We have literally hundreds of languid and effete Englishmen on our books who have found themselves alienated by a wilful lack of understanding from the modern western female and are eager to make the acquaintance of a Russian woman like **YOU!**

The English House Husband is loving and caring, and proficient in pleasing the ladies by strumming on his lyre, reciting epic poetry or generally lolling about the house in a decoratively languid manner. He will happily pen esoteric odes specially designed to entertain you when you return from a gruelling day at the factory or the office, or introduce you to the excitment of the casino as he carefully invests your hard-earned wages.

In return for all this he wants to be pampered and looked after, and for you to keep his sartorial requisites in a state commensurate with the expectations of an English gentleman.

Contact us now and within 7 days you too could be meeting up with your first date.

Phone Moscow 23 460 345 342 or visit our web site.

Somewhere out there there is an English House Husband who is looking for someone just like YOU!

www.englishhousehusbands.com

DMITRI SPATTERDOVICH MAKES EXCELLENT SPATS

Of this much a St Petersburg gentleman can be certain. But have you noticed, sir, that on particularly inclement days when the snow is splashing at you from every direction as you stroll along Nevsky Prospekt, that when you return to your chambers, the only part of your raiment that does not require immediate attention from your valet is your socks?

And why, precisely, is that, good sir? It is because, I think you will agree, your spats (purchased in all likelihood from my very own gaiter store on Ulitsa Gertsena) have done the work that they were laboriously and carefully hand-stitched to do by my seamstresses. Gentlemen, what I offer to you today is a radical innovation in gaiter and spatterdash manufacture. The all-over full body spat (patent pending) will, thanks to my revolutionary design, ensure that you return from a walk with your entire outfit as spick and span as your valet prepared it in the morning. I hereby invite you to pay me a visit at D. Spatterdovich, Ulitsa Gertsena 97, St Petersburg, for a personal demonstration of the all-over full body spat.

RESTAURANTS:
SERGEI'S BURGERS

It has often been mentioned, not without a hint of *schadenfreude*, that the former singer of English seventies pop sensation Dollar, David Van Day, is now the proprietor of a successful hamburger van in Margate. Pop fans visiting Russia will not want to miss out on a brief day trip to Ostrov, a run-down resort on the Black Sea that resembles Margate in many ways. Follow the roaming gangs of Eastern European petty criminals, and you will find yourself at a little van next to the closed-down pier which purveys an excellent meat patty in a bun. The proprietor is one Sergei Smerdyakov, the male half of the once hugely popular singing duo 'Kopek'.

Kopek had a massive hit in 1978 called "It is Very Nice to Be in Love With You". There followed two years of national tours, television appearances, tabloid intrusion, alcoholism and drug dependency. Sergei has put his pop stardom days behind him now, and is perfectly content to live life in the slow lane as a fast food chef.

Moscow's entrepreneurs are said to be interested in forming a new McDonald's-style chain of hamburger vans run by former pop stars. Adam Ant, Leo Sayer and Limahl have already been contacted for UK branches, while Demis Roussos is said to be interested in being a Greek branch.

SERGEI'S BURGERS
Next to Petrovsky Pier, Otrov
Open 24 hours

Krasnoyarsk, Russia, 27th December

When we embarked upon this wager, it was clear that the
journey would not be paved with the comforts we are
accustomed to. This much I had gleaned from browsing
through the single copy of *National Geographic* housed
in the library of the Sheridan Club - more as a
caution than for genuine literary interest. I had made
great efforts, upon setting off, to banish the memory
of the gypsy caravans, African mud huts and Japanese
capsule hotels revealed to me in those dark pages. Yet
nothing could have prepared me for the indignity of
spending the night at the waiting room of Krasnoyarsk
Railway Station. The Trans-Siberian Express was
supposed to have deposited us in Vladivostok, but an
unfortunate incident aboard the train led to us
alighting at this Godforsaken place.

With our budget now having been severely depleted and
the prospect of crossing three more continents, we saw
no alternative but to tackle this lengthy portion of
the voyage in steerage. There are few sensations
guaranteed to cut a gentleman to the quick more than
the wretched walk, sans porter, to the back end of a
train. One is forced to watch liveried porters hauling
trunkloads of fine things into the first class
carriages, while one makes one's way to where the
platform trails away into an overgrown ditch.

Nevertheless, once the train had departed, our spirits
were lifted by the glorious sight of the Russian
peasantry toiling away in the Central Russian Uplands.
Knowing that someone, somewhere was slightly poorer
than us made the hard wooden seats almost bearable.
Fortunately, a mutual accord of silence existed for the
first few hours of the journey between ourselves and
our fellow passengers. At one point Masaki disappeared,
no doubt to weep in private at the circumstances his
masters had been reduced to.

Masaki returned some thirty minutes later in the

company of an almost identical manservant. "Gentlemen," announced Masaki, "may I present to you Vladimir Petyatkin, head valet to the house of Prince Leopold Myshkin XII." Victor and I responded to the proffered bow with a discreet nod, not having the faintest idea what the inscrutable one was up to.

"I am deeply honoured to make your acquaintance," purred Masaki's Russian counterpart. "My master has avidly followed your voyage in the Russian newspapers. He begs to know if you would do him the honour of travelling with him in his Royal carriage?"

"Masaki," I croaked, trying to restrain the euphoria in my voice, "gather our luggage together instantly."

Mr Petyatkin led us through an endless quantity of railway carriages whose standards of accommodation gradually increased, until we reached a large oak panelled door. Our guide unlocked it and led us into a miniature palace. Prince Myshkin, a dainty though rather rotund fellow, was seated on an enormous ottoman. His tiny feet perched upon a plump silk cushion, he was sipping tea from a porcelain cup and saucer while several servants fussed over a large samovar in the corner. "Please, please, sit down, my friends!" said the Prince. "Won't you join me in some afternoon tea?"

It seemed our ludicrous voyage had not escaped the attention of the Russian press, and every step of our journey had been chronicled in daily reports. Our host was the scion of the exiled Myshkin dynasty, whose lives were devoted to travelling around Russia and pretending the Revolution had never happened. The pointless extravagance of our wager evidently appealed to the Prince, to the extent that he had instructed his people to find a valet identical to the image of Masaki which had appeared in an edition of *Komsomolskaya Pravda*.

Once we were installed in Prince Myshkin's carriages, our every whim was catered for. Victor and myself each had a luxurious suite of our own, with Masaki installed in his own room between them. We took all our meals with the Prince, and every day he would read us the exquisite poetry of Aleksandr Pushkin, asking for nothing in return except for us to regale him with quotations from the great English poets.

Everything was going swimmingly until somewhere around the outskirts of Krasnoyarsk. We had just joined the Prince for dinner and he was gazing out of the window at the dramatic peaks of the Urals. Standing by his side, I was moved to deliver a brief quotation from John Keats: "Like stout Cortez when with eagle eyes/He star'd at the Pacific – and all his men/Look'd at each other with a wild surmise/Silent, upon a peak in Darien."

Prince Myshkin turned to me, with uncannily eagle-like eyes. "Did you say *stout* Cortez, my friend? Are you suggesting that the girth of your host is not what it should be?"

"But of course not, your highness. I was merely extrapolating ... that is to say, I simply wanted to make a comparison with ..."

There was no further discussion. Prince Myshkin had taken great offence at my chance remark, and in between muttering about not being our "fat friend" any more, he had us all thrown off the train at Krasnoyarsk. Traumatised by the experience, and loath to go in search of an hotel in the freezing Siberian temperatures, we made camp in the waiting room of the railway station. Victor consoled me by remarking that the Prince *was* rather on the corpulent side, and sooner or later someone would have mentioned it.

ART & CULTURE:
MAD TSAR PAUL'S MUSEUM OF SNOW

FOLLOWING IN THE footsteps of the mighty architectural expansion of St Petersburg by his predecessors Peter the Great and Catherine the Great, "Mad" Tsar Paul had a lot to live up to. His single successful project was Mikhailovsky Castle, but he also managed to complete several smaller, lesser-known projects during his short reign, before being smothered to death by military conspirators. One of these is the St Petersburg Museum of Snow. Mad Tsar Paul took the time to observe the qualities of St Petersburg's frequent snowfall, coming to the conclusion that the snow differed slightly from day to day. Peter the Great would have his Alexander Nevsky Monastery and Catherine the Great her Winter Palace, but Mad Tsar Paul was determined to be remembered for his Museum of Snow.

The lavish building, in the Baroque style, took seven years to complete, and contained a hundred and seventy glass cases to house the different kinds of snow. The museum was completed in the winter of 1797 and all the vitrines filled with snow. Mad Tsar Paul had not anticipated what would happen to the snow once it was liberated from the ground, and within a few weeks the meticulously labelled glass cases all contained nothing but murky water. Within a year, even the water had evaporated.

The museum is worth a visit today, if only to observe the greatest folly of Russia's most foolish ruler. Gazing at row upon row of empty vitrines, each with its detailed description, makes for a curious experience not unlike visiting a contemporary art gallery in England.

ST PETERSBURG MUSEUM OF SNOW
Tserkovnaya Gorka Ulitsa, 27
Open Tuesday-Sunday 10am-5pm
Free entry

Frost Trouser / Tundra Chafe
(Congelation sartorius)

While frost-bite may be regarded as the king of afflictions in chilly climes (nothing is quite as impressive as returning to base camp with four twigs of charcoal where your toes used to be), the related conditions of Frost Trouser and Tundra Chafe can be safely calculated to add gravitas and credence to your tales of Arctic heroism.

Frost Trouser occurs when the perspiration from a gentleman explorer's exertions freezes solidly within the weave of his tweeds, rendering them inflexible and causing acute fatigue and muscle strain to the wearer. After prolonged walking in sub zero temperatures across the snowy wastes, Tundra Chafe can set in as a secondary condition. This occurs when the frozen trouser cloth abrades a man's nether regions, forcing him to walk side saddle.

Fig 89. Grade III Chafing

Siberian Chronicle

DECEMBER 20 DAYLIGHT EDITION. 5 KOPECS   NO. 4,865

DEEP FROZEN GULAGS FOUND

OMSK, 19TH DECEMBER:
REMARKABLE DISCOVERIES HAVE BEEN MADE UNDER THE TUNDRA OF REMOTE AREAS OF SIBERIA.

Areas previously thought to consist of nothing but solid ice-packed earth have cracked, to reveal perfectly preserved cells from Siberia's notorious gulags. Underneath dozens of metres of icy tundra, excavations have found perfectly preserved prisoners in their gulag cells, some of them dating from over a 100 years ago.

Amazed onlookers watch as a deep-frozen Daniil Kharms is revealed in an excavated Siberian gulag

Reporter Vladimir Bulyakin visited one of the excavations, where in a perfectly preserved gulag cell from 1864, Fyodor Dostoevsky had been frozen solid while hard at work on his novel The House of the Dead. Unsurprisingly, Russia's literary giant was not pleased at being disturbed. "I have already told the guards a hundred times," he said, clearly not realising he had been thawed out in the 21st century, "I am writing one of the great novels of the 19th century and I must be left in peace."

When Bulyakin explained that, due to a major ice collapse in 1864, Dostoevsky had been perfectly preserved under the tundra for 140

years, Russia's greatest writer was even more incensed. "This means that my greatest rival, Leo Tolstoy, will be long dead when my new novel is published. Curses! This was to be my finest, the one that really showed Tolstoy who was the master! Now I won't be able to see his face when he reads the reviews of The House of the Dead."

Under another collapsed section of tundra, another perfectly preserved gulag cell was found, this one containing the absurdist poet Daniil Kharms. Imprisoned in 1935 by Stalin for dissident writing, Kharms was not as outraged as Dostoevsky at being told he had been preserved until the 21st century. He was even more delighted when informed that the Soviet Union had been

dismantled. "You mean Stalin is dead? Good. Here's a poem: 'Stalin's a gonner, O ladies of Moscow. Let's go and dance with rainbows. Let's make love and chew antelopes. Let's make bras out of matchsticks and take them off! Let's sew sequins on our ears and jump into the Volga. Stalin's a gonner. Let's get gonorrhoea!'"

Once he had been properly thawed out by medical experts, Kharms was pronounced fit and healthy. Asked what career prospects he thought he would face in 21st century Russia, he commented, "Having read all the Russian newspapers and watched some television, I can see that my country has no need for another absurdist. So I plan to emigrate to a serious country such as North Korea and seek my misfortune there."

RESTAURANT:
GULAG CHIC

SINCE THE BREAK up of the Soviet Union, the system of brutal forced labour camps, Gulags, has thankfully ceased to exist in the form and scale of their Stalinist heyday, and it is amazing how swiftly times change. In a similar way to how British chefs and designers started to look to French and Italian peasant style as their inspiration in the 1960's, now in Russia, due to growing affluence, Gulag Chic has become a la mode for those in the upper echelons of Russian society with a few roubles to rub together.

The Ivan Denisovitch Restaurant And Piano Bar

Paris-trained chef, Anatoly Polyakov's first solo venture in the Western Siberian city of Tomsk. He regards Gulag Cuisine as the natural choice in an age where "we are all calorie conscious". The decor is plain brick with concrete floors and unglazed windows, which lends an ambience of authenticity to the restaurant. Portions are fashionably small and some of the menu highlights include: Paté "King Edward" avec une Salade des Pommes de Terre (with a potato garnish and black rye bread); Timbale of Rodent with Non-Specified Root Vegetable Julienne; and for pudding a delicious and novel Floor Sweepings au Chocolat (sans le chocolat).

The Solzhenitsyn Country Gulag Retreat

Solzhenitsyn's is situated in an actual disused Gulag in the remote northern town of Potopova. Although some concessions to modern standards have been made (i.e. a fully-stocked cocktail bar, sauna, jaccuzi, massage service, full central heating, 24 hour room service, etc.) the purpose of the retreat is partly educational (as it says in the brochure), giving visitors "a startling insight into the horrors of Stalin's Russia."

Dimitri Kyznetsov

Bratsk-born clothes designer Dimitri Kyznetsov in renowned for causing a stir on the world's catwalks by having his collections of gentlemen's suits made exclusively out of old beetroot sacks. This departure from the tenets of classic gents' tailoring has made him a controversial figure. Curious visitors may judge for themselves by visiting a permanent display of his suits at the Museum of Contemporary Design, Chelyabinsk.

Ulan Bator, Mongolia, 28th January

Good God! Will this torture never end? I thought I had trammelled the lowest depths of human misery that time I had mistakenly boarded the 23.15 from Euston (having unintentionally strayed from SW1) under the drunken impression that it would somehow return me to Pimlico, only to awake some hours later in Crewe. Never in my wildest dreams did I believe that a man could sink even lower, but over the past month Gustav and I have suffered indignities that defy description. How I crave the reassuring embrace of my armchair at the Sheridan.

We are currently encamped on the outskirts of Ulan Bator in a ger, a curious tent made of felt, and not dissimilar in shape to a circus big top. This has been our nightly residence for the last five weeks and the lack of running water, electricity, sanitation, and proper furnishings has ground us down to the point of despair. Today we prayed that we might see an end to it, but we have made it to town too late to book into a hotel and must rough it for one more night before being reunited with our self-esteem.

Things had taken a distinct nosedive back in Krasnoyarsk, where Masaki had adjudicated (rather arbitrarily in my opinion) that even though we had originally planned to travel as far as Vladivostok, our summary expulsion from Prince 'Fatty' Myshkin's carriage had effectively concluded that leg of the tour, making it necessary to elect a new form of transport for the onward stretch. Despite our remonstrations and pleading Masaki was completely intransigent on the matter. It is my opinion that the fellow is getting a little above himself and I half suspect that he is trying to wreak some sort of revenge for his earlier encounter with the roof rack.

The important thing was to extricate ourselves from Krasnoyarsk. Without the option of a train, Vladivostok seemed an impossibly remote destination and we therefore decided to reroute to Ulan Bator. We had already spent three quarters of our entire funds, and we were less than a third of the way through our itinerary, so the ghastly spectre of economy travel reared its head once more. Naturally, Masaki was dispatched on one of his now characteristic forays to make the arrangements.

Some hours later Masaki revealed his master plan. There was no hint of humour on his immobile features as he announced that we would be continuing the journey by yak. He had employed the services of a local yak herd to guide us through the 1000 miles of winding mountain passes that lay ahead. At first we were incredulous and enquired whether he had taken leave of his senses, but Masaki stared back placidly and replied that "even dust amassed would grow into a mountain". There was nothing more to be said.

If we had regarded ourselves as particularly inept on horseback, then yak riding in Siberia exhibited how dangerously unsuited to animal handling we really were. For those unfamiliar with the yak, imagine a bison combined with a shag-pile carpet that is in desperate need of cleaning, and you gain a pretty good impression of the beast. Although they are placid, and highly suited to performing as a pack animal, they are a little too broad to be of any great use to a rider. Thus it was that I spent most of the trip listing at an angle of 35° to the perpendicular, and on other occasions awoke from a fine malt whisky snooze to find my forehead bumping along the track, my saddle having gradually described a rotation of 180° until I was hanging upside down. Gustav on the other hand was so shocked by the humiliation of it all that he was subdued into silence for the entire first week. For a man born to overblown rhetoric and holding forth at length this was very unusual indeed. On a couple of occasions I rode alongside him and could see his lips steadily repeating the near inaudible phrase "The horror. The horror."

Throughout the long ride nothing seemed to go to plan. My ancestral suit was falling apart at the seams, and I was obliged to change into an old world war one uniform that I had brought along because I thought it might be useful for the jungle section of our trip; my hessian briefs were becoming so painful that I was forced on the advice of our guide to use some yak lard to ameliorate the condition; the strap on one of the luggage yaks broke and we lost some important supplies (including one of our pipe racks, Gustav's travel tie press and a case of Gentleman's Relish) down the side of a ravine. Our discomfort was further exacerbated when the weather took a turn for the worse and we were subjected to the first snows of the season.

By the time we reached Kyakhta on the Mongolian border even death would have been a blessed relief, but instead more humiliation was in store. The border guards on the Russian side were a pretty surly bunch who, noticing my military clothing, decided to brighten up their day with a little "sport". A Kalashnikov was waved in my face and I was frog-marched off to an interrogation room. I was only narrowly spared the rubber glove treatment (now that would have been a fate worse than Crewe) by the quick thinking of Masaki who bribed the guards at the cost of £800 from our depleted resources together with two bottles of my Macallan 25-year-old and our remaining jars of Thedgeley's marmalade.

ART & CULTURE:

THE PHLEGM WEAVERS OF ULAN BATOR

NO STAY IN the Mongolian capital would be complete without a visit to the workshops of the quite extraordinary Phlegm Weavers of Ulan Bator. These legendary craftsmen have developed their trade over centuries as a highly singular off-shoot of the Mongol practice of 'throat singing' or höömeï, a guttural style of vocalisation that may produce a unique and charming sound, but also inevitably causes singers to expectorate vastly during the course of their performance. Living in a harsh climate and undisposed to squandering a natural resource, the Mongols have learned to utilise this muculent harvest, and to convert it into a flexible yarn renowned for its versatility, durability and water-repellent qualities.

Entering the workshops for the first time the visitor might be forgiven for gaining the impression that he had accidentally walked in on a fully-blown höömeï recital or else assuming that the building he is entering is some sort of sanatorium. The noise level is deafening, but as one's ears and eyes become accustomed one cannot help but be impressed by the quality of the craft items being made. Traditionally the yarn has been used for a wide variety of products from water containers to yak blankets, and from clothing to baskets, but now the weavers

have developed items designed to appeal more overtly to the westerner. These include socks, ties and braces for the more traditional, as well as a range of travel wear for the gentleman explorer including balaclava helmets, mittens, umbrellas and thermal underwear.

Gustav Hathersedge Temple *Esq.* c/o The Sheridan Club, St James's, London SW1

```
Prime Minister Koizumi                          Presidential Suite,
Presidential Palace                                 Hotel Excelsior,
Haki-Guru, Tokyo                            Ulan Batur, Mongolia
```

January 28th

Most honoured and esteemed Sir,

News of the voyage that myself and Mr Darkwood are engaged upon is certain to have reached places even as remote as your country. You may have noted that we are travelling in the company of one of your compatriots, one Masaki Nakatake, about whom I must request your assistance. In the short time that he has been travelling with us, Mr Nakatake has proved a most efficient and willing manservant. He recently came to me in private with a rather delicate matter, which I must now put to you.

Masaki, it appears, has "a past" in Japan, the details of which he refuses to elaborate. In short, he runs the risk of being immediately impounded by the authorities upon our arrival in Japan - something which would naturally greatly inconvenience Mr Darkwood and myself. I was wondering whether you would be prepared to take him off our hands in return for a suitable replacement? I understand that there is a "price on his head", though we would be happy to waive this sum if you could supply us with a similarly po-faced Japanese manservant, whom we could pass off as Masaki upon our return to London. Without Mr Nakatake's adjudication, we stand to lose out, both financially and honourably.

I know how you lot are sticklers for concepts of honour, duty and so forth, so I am hoping for your sympathies regarding this matter.

I have the honour to remain,
Your loyal and obedient servant,

Gustav Temple

PRIME MINISTER KOIZUMI
PRESIDENTIAL PALACE, HAKI-GURU, TOKYO

29th January

Dear Mr Temple,

Prime Minister Koizumi thanks you for your letter concerning Mr Masaki Nakatake. Unfortunately he will be unable to fulfil your request at the present time. He does, however, offer you endless harmony and fulfilment for the remainder of your journey, and is pleased to enclose a small gift for Mr Nakatake.

PP. YUKO HIGOSHIKO
Personal assistant and masseuse to
His Lofty Eminence the Prime Minister

Encl: white feathers, 4

Osaka, Japan, 30th January

It took Masaki no time at all to locate a Mongolian
glider pilot capable of taking us all the way to Tokyo.
When we turned up at the designated spot in the car park
of Ulan Bator Airport we were surprised that our pilot,
a Mr Baran, had his glider right there with him. When we
asked him how he proposed to get it airborne, he smiled
and held up a length of chain with a large hook attached
to it. "Cathay Pacific," he said cryptically and
disappeared over a nearby fence.

Mr Baran came running back a few moments later,
gesticulating wildly for us to get into the glider.
Masaki bundled all our trunks and cases and the three of
us piled into the tiny aircraft. The pilot leapt into
his cockpit just as the length of chain tightened, and
with a sharp jerk we found ourselves hurtling along the
runway in the wake of a Cathay Pacific Boeing 747.

I have always been under the impression that the whole
purpose of a glider is that, once lifted into the
heavens by a willing aircraft, it then sets about the
business of gliding. But after several hours of
thrumming along behind the 747, Mr Baran made no moves
towards unchaining the glider. I glanced at Masaki,
concerned that this may disqualify the journey if we
were to use airline travel again, but his face was the
usual Noh mask of nothingness, although I thought I
detected a single bead of perspiration on his smooth,
untroubled brow.

I wondered whether this was connected to the presence
of a shadow looming over the glider, caused by the
mighty grey bulk of a military aircraft. The red
insignia on its sides identified it as belonging to the
Japanese airforce, and as we approached Tokyo's Narita
airport, it seemed determined to assist our descent.

I could also sense Victor's unease, from the gathering
pile of empty bottles around his feet. He nudged me with
his free arm and pointed at the window. Through the
scratched Perspex I could make out several rows of

Japanese soldiers with their rifles trained on the dome
of our glider. I stole another glance at Masaki,
incredulous that this po-faced automaton had anything to
do with such an "unwelcome party". Mr Baran had
unhitched the chain and the glider's own propulsion was
now taking us on an unstoppable course towards the
runway.

We were close enough to hear the soldiers cocking their
rifles when the chain suddenly tautened again. Inches
from touching down, we were lifted back into the sky by
the military plane, which soared over the tail of the
Boeing 747 and hauled us to safety.

Masaki assured us that the military aircraft was
piloted by "a friend". We were towed south to the city
of Osaka, where we landed on a small private airstrip.
A black van was waiting for us, and once Masaki had
transferred all our belongings into it, Victor and
myself were instructed to get in as well.

"Look here old man," said Victor to Masaki, swaying
uncertainly as he surveyed the dark interior of the van,
"hadn't you better give us an explanation for all this
fuss and bother?"

"The snail who leaves its shell will find it difficult
to return," Masaki replied in his usual informative
manner. "Life in danger for us. Van take to safety." How
could anyone argue with such logic?

After a short drive, the van pulled up and the driver
opened the doors. We were led through a narrow alleyway
littered with dustbins and into a metal door, which
connected us to a series of dark passageways, leading
into one of the most enchanting sets of rooms I have had
the pleasure to enter.

It appeared to be some sort of bawdyhouse, or gambling
den, or nightclub – or possibly all three. Over three
floors, each with a wide balcony overlooking the centre,
every nuance of Oriental decadence swarmed about,
impregnating the air with the intoxicating perfume of
depravity and vice. Gaudily painted Japanese ladies with
long cigarette holders roamed about like figures in a
tableau by Lautrec; upon a circular stage in the middle
of the ground floor a quartet of Philippino transsexuals

played cello, piano, viola and bassoon entirely in the nude, while a Chinese midget performed juggling tricks with spider monkeys. The ceiling was completely obscured by the unmistakable fug of opium smoke, and in the darkest recesses, men and women were sprawled upon cushions with opium pipes dangling from their mouths.

"Paradise, Oriental style," I said to Victor, and I could see from the angle of his jaw that he agreed. We were led to a table on a balcony overlooking the stage, and served with a bottle of absinth, two phials of laudanum tincture and a pair of *yen tshungs* full of high-grade opium. Masaki seemed to be recognised by several of the kimono-clad ladies, who approached him and whispered in his ear. In every instance, Masaki replied by barking at them in Japanese with a fury I had never thought him capable of.

We remained in the bordello until the early hours, and were led to our rooms while the festivities raged on. "Masaki, old thing," I ventured, when he had translated my requirements to the harlot I had selected, "perhaps this would be a good time for a brief explanation?"

"The hungry fox causes danger to chickens," was his reply.

"Thank you Masaki, that is very reassuring," I said, wincing as my wrists were shackled to the bedpost.

COCKTAILS
HOW TO MIX THEM

THE TEMPLE MARTINI

If you are hiking through the mountains of Tibet in search of a mystical experience, then you must pay a visit to Tsang Po Temple. If you are lucky, Master Shan Akahari will be tending the bar, where he is famous for his Temple Martinis. Zen monks like their Martinis exceedingly dry, and the only bottle of vermouth is kept in Master Akahari's dormitory, where he studies it daily as part of his meditation. When he comes to prepare the Dry Martini, he has understood so deeply the 'vermouth-ness' of Vermouth, that merely by meditating on the idea of vermouth in the glass, he will be able to taste it. Visitors to the Temple have claimed that they too can taste a minute glimmer of vermouth in this, the driest of Dry Martinis.

THE RECIPE:

5 parts Plymouth Gin
1 Olive
The idea of Vermouth

BY
'ROBERT'
OF THE AMERICAN BAR,
CASINO MUNICIPAL, NICE,
AND LATE OF THE
EMBASSY CLUB, LONDON

BODY ODDIFICATION

The Suit Tattoo

TRUBSHAWE'S
Oddification Rating
★ ★ ★ ☆ ☆

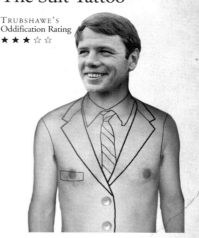

THE TRADITION OF Japanese tattooing goes back many centuries. When the Duke of York (later King George V) visited Japan in 1882, the art form was so respected that he had a dragon tattooed on his arm by the celebrated master Hori Chiyo.

The modern visitor to Japan may wish to follow in these illustrious footsteps and experiment with some of the more contemporary designs on offer. The delightful combination of tattooing and subcutaneous button implant above is guaranteed to provide the bashful chap with a swift escape route from abject nakedness and its associated realms of rudery. Sartorial elegance even when in the buff is the hallmark of the true gentleman.

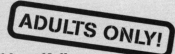
Imitating the Bamboo Plant
(Homo bambusapien mimos)

Strange social phenomena such as hikikomori
(people who withdraw from society and stay in
their bedrooms for years on end) are not
uncommon in Japan, and have a special place in
the heart of the decadent gentleman who is
himself naturally inclined to languishing in his
boudoir, sometimes for several days at a stretch,
but over the last few years the rise of a new
condition, Take no you ni (imitating bamboo),
has grown to epidemic proportions in Japan.
The gentleman traveller may wish to stop a
while on the charming parks of Tokyo, and
marvel as hordes of Take no you ni sufferers
stand exceedingly upright and very still indeed,
doing nothing at all in acute psychological
reaction to the unreasonable demands of the
overly competitive nature of Japanese society.

Fig 193. A contemplative condition

TOKYO ENQUIRER

TOKYO, 30TH JANUARY / PRICE 2¥

Shinjuku Shirkers Attack Tokyo Subway

A GANG CALLING THEMSELVES THE 'SHINJUKU SHIRKERS'
LAUNCHED AN OPIATE ATTACK ON TOKYO'S SUBWAY SYSTEM.

The Shinjuku Shirkers relax at their Tokyo HQ

At eleven o'clock in the morning, passengers on the Narita Line were suddenly overcome by the fumes of opium poppies, causing them to sit drowsily on the platforms and smile idiotically. The train remained stationary, due to the driver becoming intensely fascinated by the swirling patterns on his seat. Some of the passengers remained on the train, lying on the floor in a state of narcotic bliss, while others drifted on to the platforms to look at the colourful posters.

Members of the Shinjuku Shirkers, dressed in frilly billowing shirts and floppy hats, moved among their victims handing out copies of poems by English Romantic poets and a copy of their manifesto. The gang's aim, according to their spokesman, Mike "Lazybones" Takashi, is to put an end to the typically overworked, anxious and harassed Japanese salaryman: "These fools have been coerced into working twelve or fourteen-hour days, six days a week, in return for being allowed to take their boss to a hostess bar once a month. It is time for the salaryman to lay down his briefcase and remember the finer things in life, such as beauty, poetry and loafing."

Asked if the Shinjuku Shirkers' methods are not a little harsh, Lazybones replied, "The salaryman is so set in his busy ways that he has lost touch with his idle self. He has drifted too far from the true Japanese spirit of Zen and simplicity and become totally Americanised in his attitude to work. The only way to help the salaryman is to force him to consider the error of his ways by showing him positive examples of an alternative approach to life."

The Shinjuku Shirkers have certainly managed to persuade a sizeable group of salarymen to change their attitudes. The gang already numbers 263, and more attacks are planned with a view to tempting more recruits. Naturally Mr Takashi is not willing to reveal his strategy, but he hinted that future demonstrations would emphasise the benefits of lying about doing nothing.

As I write this from a capsule hotel, which I have decorated according to instructions on a Shinjuku Shirkers' leaflet – muslin draped over the furniture, incense burning, a bottle of wine at my elbow and a volume of verse at my feet – I can assure readers that this particular worker has been thoroughly converted.

Shanghai, China, 5th February

Oh! What I would give for an existence devoid of excitement and unnatural exertion. Back in London, I would feel resentful if I had to quicken my step whilst crossing Piccadilly, but now, here in the Far East, adrenaline-fuelled escapades, subterfuge and cloak-and-daggery are swiftly becoming a way of life.

As I pen this entry, at 10.45pm on the 3rd floor of the Imperial Hotel, I take another peak out through a crack in my curtains. Across the street I can just make out two shadowy figures lurking beneath the streetlight, smoking cigarettes and occasionally glancing up at our window. God knows who these people are or what they are after, but it is certainly a matter of concern for a gentleman.

Osaka has much to offer the refined traveller. The roads lined with gingko trees, and the perfumed teagardens, but by the time we left the city we had savoured precisely none of these delights. After our first night of languid debauchery in Masaki's pan-Oriental bordello things took a decided turn for the worse. The course of events is unclear (after all I was under the influence of copious amounts of horizontal lubricant at the time), but suffice to say, they involved a good deal of hurrying about, and being bundled into the backs of cars. At one point I'm convinced I awoke to find ourselves speeding through the city streets pursued by flashing blue lights and a chorus of wailing sirens. Thankfully I subsided back into port-fuelled reverie before my observations could be verified.

Masaki, to his credit, did finally come up with a scheme to extricate us from this madness. He had read in the newspapers about a Professor Hiroshi Nakamura of the Osaka Institute of Nautical Engineering. Gustav and I were completely nonplussed, but realised that we had very little option than to let events run their course. Our reception committee at Tokyo had convinced us that trying to leave the country by conventional routes would only end up with us mouldering away in a Japanese prison for several years.

When we tracked him down, Professor Nakamura turned out to be utterly charming, although a trifle suspect in the facial hair department, sporting as he did a long white beard sans moustache. Apparently, for some years the good professor had been working on a revolutionary mode of transport that he called a Passenger Torpedo. The Professor was delighted when Masaki volunteered us as human guinea pigs. There was only one snag. Due to a desperate need of funding for his research, the professor would only agree to accommodate us on payment of £2400. With our funds now desperately depleted this meant that we would arrive in Shanghai with precisely £32.56 to our name. As I have said, we had no alternative.

So it was that we gathered at a secret location amongst the islands and inlets of Osaka Bay at four in the morning ready for blast off. The torpedo was larger than I had imagined, and bore a worrying resemblance to an oversized bob sleigh, but on viewing the interior we realised that, though a bit snug, our passage had every likelihood of being a pleasant one. After stowing the luggage at the rear, I ensconced myself just in front of it and set about brewing up a nice cup of Lapsang Souchong in my travel teas-made before I settled down with a leather-bound copy of Mirbeau's *Torture Garden*. Unfortunately the Professor had failed to inform me of the effects of G-force and by the time we had gained the mid East China Sea my starched white shirt had been converted by the Lapsang into an artwork by the late Mr Jackson Pollock.

As we neared Shanghai Harbour and our velocity gradually diminished, it became evident that Professors Nakamura's invention had some considerable design flaws. From inside our pod we were aware of a number of collisions. It was only when, once at the quayside, we were able to slide back the hatch and observe exactly what had taken place, that we spied a trail of devastation, with enraged junk owners clinging onto their vessels in various stages of capsize. There was only one thing to do, run like the wind. We hastily removed ourselves to the safety of the Imperial and the long missed comforts of five-star accommodation.

Residing at a hotel we have no earthly means of paying for is not without some perverse satisfaction, but finding ourselves once again pursued by a nameless foe is firing up my dander to unfeasibly large proportions. Those fellows are still lurking outside and my outrage has not even been quelled by downing a bottle of Taylors Vintage 1977. In fact, with this timely instalment of Dutch courage, I feel it is time to confront those devils. After all, it is an intolerable state of affairs: an Englishmen barricaded in his own room …

1.20am. Imperial Hotel, Shanghai. Oh dear! Since downing my pen some two hours ago, I seem to have made a bit of a fool of myself. In retrospect, my first mistake was probably my dress code. Striding down to the narrow roadway below our window dressed in my nightgown and a pith helmet had not been calculated to instil respect, but by the time I had flailed my cane about my head a few times I probably made my intentions clear enough.

I had managed to land several convincing blows by the time Gustav and Masaki had rushed down, having overheard the commotion, and dragged me off my unfortunate victims. Rather embarrassingly it transpires that they had nothing to do with the Japanese authorities and were merely a couple of enthusiastic followers of our expedition. They were hoping to bag an autograph or two before our onward march. It seems they caught a great deal more than they had bargained for.

I am now unsurprisingly in the doghouse. Gustav has suggested that I "calm down a little" and has retired to his room with Masaki to plan some money making venture for tomorrow. It remains to be seen whether they will be successful.

CHINESE CUISINE

RUMOURS ABOUND CONCERNING the gastronomic extremes of the Chinese, but sad to say it is nigh impossible to find a restaurant nowadays serving fresh monkey brains straight from the skull. However, there are many other unusual delicacies available in China for the fellow with a palette for the peculiar.

BIRD'S NEST SOUP: An age-old delicacy made from swift nests, whose silk-like strands of saliva soften when cooked and resemble noodles. Overworked saliva glands produce a red nest, though the cooked white nests are the more readily available.

DOG KENNEL SOUP: Chunks of wood marinated in oyster sauce and dog hair and steamed to perfection. If you are lucky you will find some of the dog in there as well.

CAT LITTER CHOP SUEY: Exactly what it says on the tin. Served with fried rice, this dish has a subtle texture that is at once crunchy and chewy.

HOXTON FIN SOUP: The Chinese killed off all the sharks a long time ago, but they have a steady supply of trendy DJs and web designers from London's most fashionable borough, whose ironic hairstyle makes for a delicious, if a tad greasy, soup.

SNAKESKIN SUIT WAN TON: When Chairman Mao issued everyone with regulation utility wear, he didn't simply throw away all that confiscated Western-style clothing. Grab a bowl of this tasty, if a little on the starchy side, soup before the supplies run out.

ELEPHANT TAIL CHOW MEIN: It seems a pity that the whole elephant has to be slaughtered just for its tail, but what a tasty tail! Marinated in soy sauce, it acquires a delicious tender quality and is served with noodles and a garnish of deep-fried giraffe eyebrows.

Bangkok, Thailand, 20th February

I have come to the conclusion that there is no sounder investment a gentleman traveller can make than a pair of hand made kid-leather gloves. They will make all the difference between good service and no service at all. Allow me to elaborate.

We arrived at the Imperial Hotel last week with precisely £32.56 in our purse. Victor made a drunken attempt to collar one of the porters and explain that we were "those bloody famous coves you've been reading about in the papers …" It was shaping up to be an impressive pronouncement, and I rather think that Victor hoped the response would be an invitation to occupy the Presidential Suite with the compliments of the management. Alas, we will never know, for he interrupted himself mid-sentence with a sudden tumble into a potted rhododendron, losing both his dignity and the attention of the porter in one fell swoop. I instructed Masaki to deal with Victor, and marched into the hotel armed with nothing but my savoir-faire and the aforementioned gloves.

It was all fairly straightforward. The information required by the receptionist of a five-star hotel as to the solvency of a potential guest is ascertained in a glance lasting approximately three seconds; one second for each level of his raiment. I was wearing a pair of hand-tooled chestnut legates by George Cleverly, a bespoke linen suit with the unmistakable single button of Huntsman and the kid-leather gloves, all of which settled the formalities to everyone's satisfaction.

Once installed in our suite, we draped Victor over a divan, and Masaki and I put our heads squarely to the matter at hand, to wit, how long it would be before we aroused the suspicion that collectively we possessed barely enough money to have a single shirt laundered at this hotel?

"Surely whatever circle of infamy you inhabited in Osaka extends to the boundaries of this, the very Oriental capital of depravity?" I asked the inscrutable one.

"The white swan on the river …" he began, but I held up a gloved hand. "Yes, alright, enough of all that mystical jiggery pokery. I think it is time we applied some Western pragmatism to this matter. As you know, I have a fondness for gambling that has led me into some of the most singular wagers imaginable, and I propose that we find a way of putting our remaining £32.56 to profitable use. I imagine you are au courant with the casinos of this city?"

"Shanghai casinos' minimum bet one thousand Yuan."

"Alright then, but what about the less official gambling dens? Don't they have things like cock fighting or praying mantis tournaments here?"

"Master no enjoy cock fighting. Very dangerous people. Places for fighting not clean."

"Very well, I shall have to overlook the personal hygiene issues. I think you'll agree that we are faced with very few alternatives. Masaki, prepare my special inside-out suit."

Before embarking on this voyage, I had instructed my tailor to fashion me a special suit for use in emergencies such as this. I predicted finding myself in unusual scrapes and scenarios that would require me to travel incognito, mingling with the common man. Mr Saxby had therefore constructed me an elaborate disguise, using traditional tailoring materials assembled in reverse order. The coarse lining canvas was on the outside, stitched together to resemble a cheap off the peg suit, while a fine worsted was used on the inside, with all Mr Saxby's famous detailing placed where only the wearer could appreciate them.

Once dressed, I resembled the sort of fellow one might purchase some shoelaces from on Victoria Embankment. Masaki, also needing to disguise himself as a bona fide visitor to the seamy side of Shanghai, simply borrowed Victor's suit, leaving our slumbering companion discreetly attired in some hotel towels and a shower cap.

Masaki led me along some narrow lanes that flanked the grand artery of the Nanking Road. Chickens, rather than people, seemed to have the run of the place; around every corner we were assailed by a squawking coop of hysterical poultry, and I soon understood why the coolies wore such voluminous straw hats. I thanked whichever god lorded over this chaotic land that I was wearing my inside-out suit and not something more precious, for when we finally reached our destination my shoulders sported a pair of epaulettes composed of chicken ordure.

Masaki had led me to some unspeakably vile den of iniquity behind a street market. We entered a species of dilapidated warehouse, where in a clearing among the packing cases we saw what we required: seventy or eighty men clamouring around a small arena in the dust, where two cockroaches were attempting to rip each other's limbs off. "How charming," I muttered to Masaki. "Who needs Monte Carlo when you can have this?"

Betting on cockroach fights doesn't differ greatly from betting on pugilism, except that it is considerably easier to weigh up the combative potential of sixteen stone of brute proletarian than something you might scrape off the sole of your shoe. After betting on a dozen or so fights, we emerged into the twilight a few hundred pounds in pocket. I suggested hot footing it to the nearest proper casino, but Masaki assured me that we still had nowhere near the minimum bet to allow us to enter such a place.

"Masaki have better idea. Now enough money for junk. We go Bangkok tomorrow. Bangkok have better casinos. No minimum bet."

Our few hundred pounds secured us a moderately comfortable journey across the South China Sea on a junk. What remained of our cockroach fight winnings I spent on the Thai bride sweepstake in Bangkok, rapidly turning £48.32 into just over ten thousand pounds. The only thing that bothered me about this timely visitation from Lady Luck was that I had not invented the sport myself.

Gustav Hathersedge Temple *Esq.* c/o The Sheridan Club, St James's, London SW1

The Manager   The Bridal Suite,
Bangkok Weddings   Bangkok Radisson,
Kowloon Street, Bangkok 20934   Thailand

24th September 2003

To whom it may concern,

Allow me to introduce myself. I am Gustav Temple of Pimlico, London, bon vivant,
man of letters and professional gambler. It has come to my attention that your
fair city of Bangkok enjoys a reputation as a rather sporting city. Indeed, many
of the most passionate gamblers I have encountered in London have often said that
in Bangkok a man can lay a wager on just about anything.

   I wonder whether you would be interested in participating in a new gambling
venture that I propose to establish here in Bangkok? The Thai Bride Sweepstake
would function as follows. Ten forthcoming weddings between Thai ladies and
Western men would be "in the running", with punters being invited to bet on the
marriage they think will have the shortest duration. It is a well-documented fact
that most marriages between large, unattractive, unpleasant Western divorcees and
pretty 19-year-old Thai girls with no command of English usually last somewhere in
the region of one to two weeks. I myself would take the role of bookmaker,
calculating the odds based on the unsuitability of each couple. I am hoping that
you will provide me with the details of forthcoming weddings, as well as the
personal details of those involved, in order to create a form table.

   Please contact me at the above address to discuss this matter further.

I have the honour to remain,
Your obedient servant,

Gustav Temple

BANGKOK WEDDINGS
Kowloon Street
Bangkok 20934
Tel 00989 232 482
The second happiest day of your life awaits you with a lovely Thai bride!

25th September 2003

Dear Mr Temple,

Thank you for your recent letter. Your idea is very interesting, but unfortunately it is not
original. There are already several Thai bride sweepstakes in Bangkok, one of which we
organise ourselves. Please visit one of our booths in the Pyongpen district for full details.

Thank you for thinking of us,

Mari Tomaloon
Manager
Bangkok Weddings

ART & CULTURE:
SHADOW SMOKERS

MANY VISITORS TO Thailand will fail to travel beyond the louche environs of Bangkok, which is a terrible pity, as they miss out on the phenomenal Shadow Smokers of Surat Thani as a consequence. Whilst most self-respecting Englishmen pride themselves on an ability to blow a smoke ring or two, the shadow smokers have taken the skill of sculpting tobacco smoke into a rare art form. From behind a back-lit screen a succession of competing shadow smokers will attempt to outdo each other with the skill and complexity of their creations. A deep intake of smoke is followed by a long exhalation and then almost miraculous-

ly the silhouetted figures of animals, temples, local deities and attractive young ladies appear upon the screen to the delight of the awe-struck audience.

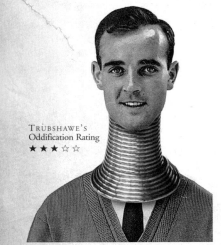

TRUBSHAWE'S
Oddification Rating
★ ★ ★ ☆ ☆

BODY ODDIFICATION
The Giraffe Neck

THE NECK RINGING propensities of the Karen Padaung tribe of the Myanmar border in Thailand may be regarded by some as inappropriate for the sober streets of London, but those prepared to step off the treadmill of conformity often find that there are plenty of benefits that may be reaped as a consequence. By lengthening his neck by some 8 inches this young man will find that he stands out from the crowd at cocktail parties and is never deprived of a grandstand view on visits to the theatre or cinema. He instinctively knows he has made the right decision even if it does mean that he constantly gets joshed for resembling Professor Plum from a game of Cluedo.

Camardenshire Films Presents a Narcissus Production

Starring
REX HUNGERSTRÖM
in a role of breathtaking decadence

and
AUBREY HEARTBURN
as
a rum cove with
a terrible secret
and a penchant for
women's clothing

"Sumptuous and
sinful. ★★★★"
Gentleman's
Film Quarterly

"Bejewelled
depravity"
The Pimlico
Recorder

MY FAIR LADYBOY

18

**NOW SHOWING AT THE
BANGKOK ARTS CINEMA**

Pontianak, Indonesia, 28th February

In Bangkok, shortly after his win on the Thai Bride Sweepstakes, Gustav and I set about relieving ourselves of large chunks of our newly acquired fortune. He decided to spend the next 24 hours in the Excelsior Thai Grooming Parlour having every bodily requirement catered to (sometimes several times over). I, unfortunately, had more unpleasant matters to attend to. It had come to that point – the point that three generations of Darkwoods had looked to with dread. It was time to say goodbye to the ancestral suit and to purchase a number of replacements. Ever since Masaki had unforgivably "borrowed" my raiment in Shanghai I had been struggling with Brillo pad and pumice stone to remove an unsightly build up of what smelt uncannily like hen excrement from about the shoulders and back of the jacket. The cloth had now worn through in several places and it was lamentably time for change.

I had it on good authority that Bangkok boasts a large array of skilled, swift and reasonably priced tailors willing to produce clothing to precise specifications. Before consigning "the ancestral" to the annals of history, I got one such fellow, Mr Kim, to take its measurements and to produce, as far as humanly possible, three exact replicas. Although I detected that my compatriots were not quite as moved as I was by the pathos of the occasion, Gustav and Masaki were decent enough to accompany me down to the harbour where I performed a brief "burial at sea" ceremony. Gustav kindly recited some poignant lines from Jules Barbey d'Aurevilly's "On Dandyism" whilst I gently launched "the ancestral" out onto the waves afloat a bamboo raft garlanded with jasmine blossom and illuminated with candles.

Considering our newly found wealth and my recent bereavement, one might suppose that Masaki, on being dispatched in the usual way to seek out onward transport, would have considered this a nice juncture for selecting a particularly salubrious mode of carriage. Not a bit of it. Instead and for reasons best known to himself, he decided to saddle us with one of his most challenging 'proposals' to date.

At Masaki's behest, we were swiftly conveyed by taxi to an arena cheerily named The Bangkok Sea World Experience, and led by one of the keepers to a large outdoor swimming pool.

"I can't see much by the way of transport here," observed Gustav leaning inquisitively over the water's edge.

At that point, the head of a fish the size of a Morris Minor appeared from the depths of the pool and rose to a height of 16 feet before plunging back into the water. "We travel by killer whale," said Masaki matter-of-factly.

Gustav turned towards us. He had been hit by the full brunt of the tidal wave and stood dripping like a snowman caught in a rapid thaw. His panama had been turned into a plant pot on his head and he was not happy. "N-never. I would rather be eaten alive by dormice," was all he could bring himself to utter.

For the rest of the afternoon Gustav shut himself away in his room and all that could be heard was the occasional muttered oath, the hissing of damp trouser in press and the mechanical whirring of his Trumpington Patent Hat Steamer.

For some reason, when Masaki made one of his transport "suggestions", it seemed strangely impossible to demur. All there was to be done, therefore, was to come up with a plan that would at least minimise the worst effects of hypothermia and drowning. I thought I would visit Mr Kim once more to consult him regarding suitable attire for our crossing. Mr Kim assured me that it would be eminently possible to construct a pair of durable, waterproof and stylish travel suits made entirely out of latex rubber. Within 24 hours the chap had whisked up two of the most singular outfits imaginable. He had skilfully reproduced the exact cut and elegance of our suits, together with razor sharp trouser creases and perfectly proportioned lapels, but entirely modelled from rubber. The headwear consisted of a moulded latex trilby the lower rim of which was sympathetically welded atop a conventional rubber diving hood. For shoe protection he had tailored two elegant pairs of over-galoshes finished off with an attractive brogue design. Thankfully when Gustav saw our new outfits, he was sufficiently impressed to deprive the dormice of their repast and have a stab at whale riding in their stead.

Meanwhile Masaki, possibly in order to make reparation for his tarnished relations with his masters, had acquired a majestic pair of ceremonial Thai thrones, which were to be secured on our whales with lengths of latex strapping. It turned out that there were three whales available: one each for Gustav and myself (and some of our personal belongings), and a third that would serve as transport for Masaki, the whale keeper and the remainder of our luggage. Masaki and the trainer had opted for more conventional wet suits, which did not cut such a dash as our own attire. I can only speculate over the picturesque spectacle that we must have made as we headed out to open seas, each of us enthroned upon the arching backs of our aquatic steeds as they rhythmically leapt through the briny on our course to Borneo.

We had selected Pontianak as a destination as it is known as "the city of the Equator" and Gustav and I were eager to experience the raucous shenanigans associated with "crossing the line". We were not to be disappointed. Pontianak lies on the Kapuas River where many houses are built over the water and are connected with each other by wooden bridges. On gaining shore the local dignitaries, cognisant of our journey, plied us with goblets brimming with various 'medicinal' herbs, and we were merrily transported about the walkways by a burly fellow dressed as Neptune, and a whole menagerie of locals decked out in costumes that seemed to be entirely made out of shells and seaweed.

I have suggested to Gustav that we stay here for a further four weeks, but he sadly reminded me that time is pressing and we must shortly find new transport for our onward journey.

Tate Borneo

The Tate Gallery is proud to announce the opening of a new gallery of contemporary art in the stylishly refurbished interior of an abandoned Dayak longhouse. Our first exhibition is an installation by local artist Fatar Utama. He has placed against one wall of the gallery a row of coconut shells, while opposite them sits a pile of empty cans of Coca-cola.

Utama's principal themes are identity, nationality and alienation. Within the 'altered' walls of the longhouse (the traditional Dayak homestead) he has created a visual dialogue between 'tradition' and concepts of proprietorial intervention. By showing us what was, what is, and what will be, Utama invites the viewer to question his own visual history – in effect, he is creating a map of the human journey, adding a playful, mischievous nod to post-structuralist concepts of spatial unity.

Tate Borneo
Jl Khatulistiwa 24
Pontianak

Exhibition runs until 3rd September

www.tateborneo.com

THE HEADHUNTERS OF BORNEO

IN THE WILDS of the Borneo jungle there exists a tribe with relatively recent origins, who have adapted the ancient tradition of headhunting to the modern world. The Yupi tribe is a rigidly hierarchical society, with one's social station being determined by the printing quality of one's business card and the amount of influence held with the maitre d' at the village's single brasserie-style restaurant. The Yupi traditional dress consists of a navy blue loincloth supported by strips of red-dyed material looped over the shoulders, while the neck is adorned with lengths of rush tied in a fat Windsor knot.

The Yupi tribe occupy themselves principally with the business of headhunting. After spending several hours grooming themselves, they set off to visit tribes in other villages, where they attempt to persuade high-ranking tribesmen to join the Yupi. The recruitment ritual usually takes place at the best long house in town, where the targeted fellow is lavished with gourmet food, vintage wines and attractive pay packages.

BODY ODDIFICATION

Extended Earlobes

TRUBSHAWE'S
Oddification Rating
★ ★ ★ ★ ☆

THE DAYAK WOMEN of West Kalimantan have a charming tradition of extending their earlobes to unfeasible lengths through the application of heavy earrings. A chap with a sense of adventure and an ability to brazen it out at dinner parties may wish to emulate such behaviour. In Dayak circles the elongation of the lobe is regarded as ravishingly attractive, but even if you find that their aesthetic sensibilities lose something in the translation on your return to England, the resultant loop of flesh will provide an image-conscious fellow with handy storage space for essential grooming items such as a shaving brush, a cut-throat razor or (as illustrated here) a comb.

COCKTAILS
HOW TO MIX THEM

THE HORN MARTINI

There is thought to exist only a single herd of Javanese rhinoceros on the planet. One of the reasons for their small number is the popularity of their horns, which the Javanese believe to be an aphrodisiac. George Rumphius, a 17th century European traveller to the East Indies, discovered that it also cured snakebite and was believed to alleviate the pain of giving birth. He put the horn's supposed aphrodisiac qualities to the test by creating his own special blend of gin, Vermouth and powdered rhino horn, and was pleased to note his increased success with the local ladies when he served them with his Horn Martini in his tent on the island of Bali. Visitors to modern-day Bali will find it easier to find a pint of snakebite than a Horn Martini, but is worth asking village elders, who seem to have several attractive young wives, for advice on where to find one.

THE RECIPE:

7 parts Booths Gin
2 parts Vermouth
3 parts powdered rhinoceros horn
8 parts smooth talk
BY
'ROBERT'
OF THE AMERICAN BAR,
CASINO MUNICIPAL, NICE,
AND LATE OF THE
EMBASSY CLUB, LONDON

Orang, M'lord?

BRITISH ZOOLOGIST PROFESSOR Algernon Floot (now retired and living in Pontianak) has spent over three decades of his life in the rainforests of Borneo and Sumatra studying the lifestyle of the orang-utang and acting as a passionate advocate for preservation of their natural habitat.

Each year the destruction of acres of rainforest has meant that dozens of orang-utangs have been "displaced" and their only chance of survival is to be housed into special reserves.

Now, Professor Floot, so accustomed to prolonged disputes with logging companies, finds that he himself is at the centre of a growing controversy. It has come to light that when he retired, unbeknownst to fellow researchers, Floot decided to "adopt" one of his rescued animals, an 8 year-old male named Sintang, and train him up as a manservant.

Outraged members of the Kalimantan Institute of Wildlife Research are now claiming that

Sintang is still the property of the institute and as such should be returned forthwith.

When interviewed on the veranda of his Pontianak home, Professor Floot was keen to explain his position.

"When we first rescued Sintang he was in a terrible condition. I immediately developed a rapport with the little chap and vowed that I would look after him for as long as I could. On retiring last year, taking him with me was the only option."

The institute claim that dressing Sintang up in a butler's uniform and requiring him to perform the duties of a manservant is depriving the orangutang of its natural dignity, but the Professor is robust in defending himself.

"Sintang is extremely happy in his present employment and gets to wear only the best tailored cloth. Surely no one in their right mind would suggest that sleeping on straw in a cage full of your own ordure and living off a diet of vegetables can be described in any way as 'dignified'. Sintang performs his ironing, hoovering and cocktail making duties with aplomb and, other than his rather annoying habit of swinging from the light fittings, we get along just fine."

Professor Floot exchanges a few pleasantries with his trusty 'manservant' Sintang as he serves up the first martini of the day.

Australasia

Perth, Australia, 6th March

The period of recuperation from our voyage across the Gulf of Siam took several days, principally consisting of the application of Trussington-Spear's Sartorial Embrocation to banish the effects of synthetic fibres on the Temple epidermis. My great grandfather, the late Theodore Temple of Belgravia, would be turning in his unmarked grave in Southend if he knew that a descendant of the noble family of Temple, an unbroken line of exquisitely attired Macaronis, dandies, fops and men-about-town, had travelled to Borneo in a rubber suit. I devoted the rest of my time to consulting our collection of world maps to devise possible methods of reaching our next destination, Australia. A distance of some 1,600 miles separated us from that low-lying continent, and I made it quite clear to Masaki that the greatest efforts must be made to maintain standards. "No more bloody great fish, please, Masaki," I said. The temptation was to squander all our remaining cash on a first class airfare to Sydney and bugger the consequences, but Masaki pointed out that we might need to use our single aeroplane journey on a much longer route farther afield. "But many other ways to fly, Master," he said, enigmatically. "If you're thinking of hoisting us to an albatross or something," I protested, "you can ruddy well forget it." You have to be firm with these Orientals, or they quite simply take advantage.

But it turned out that what Masaki was driving at, in his kimono-unravelling way of speaking, was that we could always make the journey by helicopter. "An absolutely wizard notion, you old cherry blossom!" I declared. "Let's go and find the town's heliport."

It soon became clear that we would have to look farther

afield for such a trapping of Western decadence as a
heliport. I studied the map more closely, and saw that
Borneo is not the island nation it appears at first. Its
territory is shared by the Malaysians, the Indonesians
and the citizens of the Sultanate of Brunei Darussalam,
whatever they choose to name themselves. When I
consulted Trubshawe for a potted history of Brunei, the
phrases "oldest continuous monarch in the world" and
"British protectorate" sprang out at me, and when I
alighted on the name "His Highness Sultan Pengiran Muda
Mahkota Hassanal Bokliah", I knew I had to meet the
Sultan of Brunei.

"Right Masaki, begin packing instantly and rouse that
Darkwood. We're leaving for Brunei on the next available
rickshaw."

It was a long journey through lush jungle, a trifle on
the humid side but pretty enough to look at. It didn't
occur to me to send news of our imminent arrival at the
Sultan's palace until halfway through Sarawak. At the
British Consul's office in Sibu I was introduced to a
novel new form of communication not dissimilar to the
old-fashioned telegraph. I was told to type my message
on a species of typewriter, which the Consul said he
would send to the Sultan as soon as the "server" was
functioning. I took this to mean the cataleptic Chinaman
dozing on a rattan chair in his garden. We pressed on
with our journey, safe in the knowledge that our wire
would reach the Sultan in good time to announce our
arrival at his palace.

It came as quite a surprise, then, to hear the whirring
of a helicopter over our heads somewhere on the
outskirts of the Sarawak-Brunei frontier. Our rickshaw
driver screamed, leapt from his saddle and disappeared
into some nearby foliage. Victor and I sat patiently in
the back of the rickshaw, watching the chopper's blades
whipping the palm tress into a frenzy as it landed in a
field, wondering what Old Mother Providence was going to
throw at us now.

A tall, olive-skinned fellow, dressed in an immaculate
white suit of a military cut topped with a pith helmet
with feathers on it, emerged from the helicopter and

approached our rickshaw. "Mr Temple and Mr Darkwood, I presume?"

A few minutes later we were landing at the private heliport of the Sultan of Brunei, who, having received our communiqué almost as soon as it was sent (don't quite understand how) had sent one of his helicopters to pick us up. News seems to travel fast in this part of the world, and reports of our escapades had reached the Sultan via the local newspapers and his contacts in the killer whale breeding world.

We were treated to a lavish champagne reception and dinner. Our host was the most congenial of Sultans I have had the pleasure of meeting. We were gradually learning that peoples of so-called uncivilised nations seem to genuinely understand the nature of nobility, displaying it with a grace that would put to shame the pompous oafs who litter the reading room of the Sheridan during recess at the House of Lords.

We stayed the night in the opulent but tasteful chambers, noting that the Sultan had not allowed his taste to lapse into Oriental vulgarity. During breakfast the following morning, the Sultan offered his assistance for the next leg of the journey. "You would do me a great honour if you allowed my helicopter pilot to take you to Australia. I would advise you to choose Perth, on the western seaboard. That way you shall not have to tolerate the Australian people for any length of time. I can assure you that their coarseness will be as intolerable to you as it was to me."

"For us, it seems, who supped together …" I began, about to leave the Sultan with a choice quote from Browning. Just in time, I recalled my experience with Prince Myshkin, and stopped myself before putting my foot in it again. We bid a fond farewell to our charming host, and once again took to the skies for the next leg of the voyage, arriving in Perth in considerably more style than our previous, aquatic mammalian journey had permitted.

NATURAL HISTORY:
THE LYRE SPIDER

THE AUSTRALIAN 'BUSH' is no place for a gentleman, and when in the Antipodes one should keep a sharp look-out at all times for the wide range of gruesome arachnids that are said to dwell there. Several types of spider, particularly the funnelweb, redback or white-tail are highly poisonous, whilst others, namely the lyre spider, come close to giving the genus a good name. The lyre spider is virtually unique in its habit of weaving its web entirely out of vertical threads within the fork of two branches. To attract its mate the male will secure itself to the outer string of its 'lyre' and strum nonchalantly upon the instrument for several hours until the vibrations arouse the attention of a passing female. Her receptiveness at this point depends very much on the dexterity of the strumming and the nimbleness of the little jigs that the spider will enact sporadically throughout the performance.

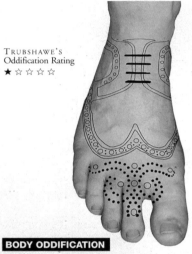

TRUBSHAWE'S
Oddification Rating
★ ☆ ☆ ☆

BODY ODDIFICATION

The Inner Brogue

THE ART OF tattooing was unknown in the western world prior to Captain Cook's first jaunt to the South Pacific in 1769. Polynesians, Hawaiians and Maoris indulged in the practice for both decorative and religious reasons. The spiritual origins of marking one's skin with needle and ink are now rekindled, with this 20th century classic. 'Finding the inner brogue' is arguably the most important mission a gentleman can indulge in. By having a traditional brogue design indelibly applied to his feet this man signifies to one and all that the high quality of his footwear is merely the external signifier of a psyche brimming with transcendentalism.

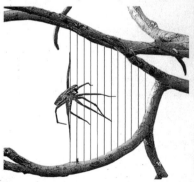

THE BORDER NEWS

All sizes available e.g.
GARAGES
20x11x8 $1450
20x20x8 $2060
40x24x9 $3730

SHEDS
40x24x9 $3160
60x30x12 $5590
100x50x16 $19185

Ask about Free Kitchen Dresser Offer

COLORPANEL

FREE DELIVERY

Gold Lic. No.27248

BORDER NEWS — WEEK COMENCING MONDAY   Vol XI No. 20

Man Builds Shed

LIGHTING RIDGE, 5TH MARCH:
Ralph Sellwood, much-loved logger and
President of the Boggabilla Town & Country
Club, has built himself a new shed.

RUMOURS OF MR SELL-WOOD'S plans to build a new shed have been circulating the district for the last few months. His old shed was beginning to look a bit tired and shabby, and everybody knew that "Old Ralph" was having difficulties with storage recently. Nick Greiner, owner of Agri-Ware in Greenbah Road, said he'd been concerned where Mr Sellwood was going to put the sixteen tins of tractor paint that he purchased last Thursday.

But when Mr Sellwood added 75 planks of timber, six hundred nails and a hundredweight of creosote, Greiner knew that the old cobber was up to something. "No-one spends that kind of money on materials unless they got some serious shed-building ideas," said Mr Greiner. "Last feller who bought that much timber was Pete Stanger, and look what he went and did. He went and built himself a bloody great shed!"

When I went over to Ralph Sellwood's farm myself to get it from the horse's mouth, there was no reply at the door. Funny, I thought, Old Ralph should be busy putting the finishing touches to his shed. I could plainly see

a timber edifice under construction in the yard, right where the old shed had been, but there was no sign of Ralph anywhere.

The mystery was cleared up when I looked at my watch and realised it was Sunday! Old Ralphie would be down at the church, wouldn't he? I waited about half an hour, maybe forty-five minutes, and then the old dingbat finally showed up. "Hey there Ralphie, what's all this about you building a new shed?"

He invited me inside for a beer and told me all about it. It seems that recently, just as Nick Greiner had suspected, Ralph was having trouble storing all his bits and pieces in that old shed of his: "You should've seen it, mate. I had tools piled so high I couldn't reach some of them, and parts of my old tractor I couldn't even recognise. Something had to be done."

I asked Old Ralphie if he'd show me his new shed, and he said yes. We walked across the yard and up to the shed, which wasn't yet finished. I could see Ralphie had opted for a two-windower, with a nice solid door with a lock. "Well, you can't be too careful these days, mate. Remember that time

Ralph Sellwood: 'Don't go pissing on my shed, mate!'

Rick Galman had all his sloper blades stolen from his shed? I still reckon it was them fellers from Dirrabandi who live in that house without a shed near the river."

I agreed with Ralph that security was an issue we all had to deal with nowadays. "I notice you haven't got a dog, Ralphie. Ever considered a bit of canine protection?"

"No, mate, I haven't," he said. "I can't stand the damn creatures, all that barking and the mess they make. I can't have a bloody great dog pissing all up the walls of my shed, can I mate?"

Well, looking at Ralph Sellwood's marvellous new shed, I had to agree. You wouldn't want a dog urinating all over it.

NATIONAL FESTIVALS:
BARBIE MARDI GRAS

OF THE MANY and varied festivals taking place throughout the year in the Southern Hemisphere, the Australian Barbie Mardi Gras ranks among the most diverting. On 16th July every year, the streets of every major town and city are filled with a procession of floats representing the elements of that traditional Antipodean repast, the barbecue. Giant chicken drumsticks dance with ten-foot sausages, while the men drink vast quantities of tinned beer and the ladies sip plastic cups of warm white wine.

The parades culminate in a ritual tournament held in the main square. Men representing the "Barbie chefs", wielding giant spatulas and two-pronged forks, chase other men dressed as barbecue ingredients to try and puncture their skins. As the sun sets, the air begins to fill with the delicious smell of smouldering charcoal and burning meat, as a thousand barbecues are ignited over the town for what the locals refer to as "a Barbie the size of bladdy Tasmania". European visitors are advised to dine with extreme caution, however. With all the beer consumed and the poorly-lit barbecues, what appears to be a very well-done kangaroo steak can often turn out to be completely raw on the inside.

BARBIE MARDI GRAS
July 17th, annually,
Australia

LET'S SPEAK AUSSIE, MATE!

AUSTRALIAN, THOUGH SUPERFICIALLY similar to English, should not deceive the British visitor. Here are some common phrases one is likely to encounter during a visit "down under" and their rough English translation:

Strewth cobber, that's a ripper pair of strides!
I say old chum, I am very impressed with the quality of your sub-pelvic tailoring.

There's no need to get so spewin' over a few mozzies!
You appear to have become unreasonably perturbed at the infestation of mosquitoes residing in your hat.

I'll eat my grundies if you're not a pommy bastard!
All the evidence before me would suggest that you are an Englishman.

Take a squizz at that boomer!
Behold that rather oversized kangaroo currently heaving into view.

Buy us a coldie, mate, I'm dry as a dead dingo's donger!
I wonder whether I could prevail upon you to purchase me a glass of beer, for I am feeling rather parched.

No need to come the raw prawn, mate, I'm no bushranger.
Your hostile attitude is incommensurate with my social status, sir, for I am not the disreputable type you seem to take me for.

Holy dooley, I've chundered on my grundies!
Good grief, I have vomited all over my undergarments!

Calcutta, India, 12th April

Only when one has traversed the terrible hinterlands of hell can one truly appreciate the pastures of Elysium. I am currently enjoying one such verdant pasture, sitting drowsily in a roomy armchair delicately sipping a Bombay Saphhire Gin and tonic from a cut glass tumbler in the Bengal Lancer Bar of the Sutanati Grand Hotel, Calcutta. It is at least some comfort that the depths to which we have been obliged to sink during the course of this monstrous journey have served to accentuate the all too rare moments of pleasure.

We had received intelligence from our friends in Brunei that the Australians, being a simple people enamoured of outdoor pursuits, had taken our peregrinations to their hearts. Although Gustav is usually far more sanguine about "publicity" than I am, even he had misgivings that in the Antipodes we would find ourselves press-ganged into a depressing circus of "beach parties" and the "barbies". We therefore decided to touch the helicopter down in the open farmland just north of Perth and travel into the centre by a less conspicuous means.

Our pilot may have been enthusiastic, but he evidently lacked some of the finer nuances of helicopter craft – namely, landing technique. On our descent into a seemingly ideal meadow, we unexpectedly came into contact with some metal object or other, and more or less stumbled onto God's good terra firma. This may not have been Perth central, but we were not without our own exclusive reception party. A red-faced farmer was tugging at the door within seconds of our landing.

Gustav was the first to the hatch. "Salutations, dear thing. We bring glad tidings from the Motherla ..."Gustav was cut short as the blackguard grabbed his lapels with a pair of raw beef fists.

"You pommie poofter, you gone an' landed on me dunny."

Gustav, despite his innate cowardice, was understandably riled by such an assault and impressively rose to the occasion. "Unhand me sir, or there will be the devil to pay". As I was still safely ensconced in the helicopter, full of Dutch courage and in no immediate danger, I felt moved to support my colleague.

"Push off at once you ruffian, or Gustav will feel compelled to engage you in a duel" I cried.

Gustav gave me an unmistakably withering glance over his left shoulder. "Yes a duel" he repeated with less than enthusiasm.

"Fair dinkum, mate, a spot of bonza aggro will do me fine," was the reply.

Judging from the available evidence, we surmised that our new acquaintance was mightily displeased at our arrival on his farm as we had inadvertently demolished his outdoor latrine in the process. After a good deal of altercation in which various means of settling the dispute were discussed, finally the suggestion of boomerang was forwarded. Having seen such a thing in the cinema in his youth, Gustav readily consented.

The duelling court was hastily assembled. Masaki acted as Gustav's second and Brett (our farmer) nominated his wife as his.

I dropped a handkerchief in order to signal the beginning of the bout, but unfortunately lost my balance, tumbling into a shallow ditch in the process. From my recumbent position I witnessed the contest.

Brett was the first to throw. The boomerang described a perfect arc narrowly missing the side of Gustav's head. Gustav visibly relaxed at this miss and rose an inch or two in defiance. Sadly he was not readied for the return of the boomerang, which reappeared unexpectedly from the rear striking his trilby and sending it tumbling it into the dust.

Enraged beyond measure my plucky compatriot took aim and threw. Practiced in fencing and marksmanship he may have been, but in boomeranging, unfortunately not. The bent wood obscenity took a disappointing 45 degree dive towards the ground, but then miraculously struck a small rock, bounced upwards and ricocheted off a nearby telegraph pole making contact with Brett's lower jaw region at an impressive velocity. He was out for the count.

Whatever you may think about the crude and primitive people of Australia they are not without their own peculiar form of decency. Brett, when he came round, seemed genuinely impressed by Gustav's good luck and offered to help us with our onward journey. It transpired that Brett's brother Bryce was a seasoned seafarer and could arrange safe passage to Calcutta.

To cut to the chase, within 48 hours we were setting sail from Perth Harbour aboard a fine Kontiki raft. For those enamoured of history, the first kontiki expedition was undertaken in 1947 by the Norwegian scientist and ethnologist Thor Heyerdahl, on a rather foolhardy journey of 3000 miles across the Pacific on a raft made of balsawood. Kontiki rafting is now a highly popular "sport" in Australia and ideally suited to the outdoor-loving Antipodeans. Our journey would add an additional 1000 miles to the length of Heyerdahl's voyage but we were not ready to be beaten by Scandinavians, and we were further encouraged by Bryce's revelation that his kontiki was equipped with the modern luxury of a powerful outboard motor. This would mean that we could make Calcutta in only 4 weeks rather than Heyerdahl's twelve on the Pacific.

As you may well imagine bobbing about in the Indian Ocean for a month on a piece of balsawood leaves a lot to be desired by way of home comforts and I fear I may have overdone it a bit on consuming the consciousness repellent – the whisky flowed like – well, whisky. Words cannot do justice to the combined horrors of sunstroke, storm and shark attack. In the latter category I still feel a trifle guilty over an unfortunate incident in which Bryce lost his left arm from the elbow down to a passing Great White. I had asked our skipper to retrieve a half-consumed bottle of Lagavulin that had carelessly slipped from my fingers. Under the circumstances Bryce was very understanding and made light of his loss, but I could tell that his wound was smarting a bit more than he let on. My guilt was exacerbated when he unfortunately died 24 hours after docking in Calcutta – a terrible loss. I was moved to write to his wife sending her a compensatory postal order for 15 guineas together with the contents of his trouser pockets.

Vic Darken

BODY ODDIFICATION

Pipe Piercings

TRUBSHAWE'S
Oddification Rating
★ ★ ★ ☆ ☆

PUSHING KNITTING NEEDLES through the side of one's face is an outré pastime much favoured by the itinerant fakirs of India, but a resourceful traveller should not be overly hasty to pooh-pooh such behaviour just because at first glance it appears exreme and frighfully un-British. With a little ingenuity, cheek piercings may easily be adapted to the needs of an Englishman. Twin perforations will allow for the luxury of dual pipe smoking without a consequent demobilisation of the mouth, leaving it free for witty conversation, gormandising and love.

Lassitude Fever
(Lassitus langourum)

This is a viral infection that exclusively affects the ex-pat community during the stifling humidity of the Monsoon season. The infection is believed to be carried by Asian water vole and transmits itself through insufficiently clean water. First symptoms occur when the patient is seen to swoon on a chaise longue for hours at length, the back of the right hand firmly clasped against the forehead, rambling on in a delirious manner about filthy wea-

Fig 71. Quinine-based remedies found most effective.

ther and Blighty . The second stage sees the patient perspiring terribly and working up a tremendous thirst. At this point, he should on no account be administered water as it could possibly contain more contaminants, but instead be offered several stiff gins and tonic. Amelioration from this point is generally surprisingly swift.

Baghdad, Iraq, 10th July

Calcutta was a curious place, reminiscent at once of Edwardian England and the Whitechapel district of London. Among the teeming hordes of busy Kolkotans ferreting about the place in their colourful clothes, there occasionally appeared an immaculately dressed Indian clutching a British newspaper and smoking a pipe with an abstracted air. The Indians have assimilated all that is great and reassuring about English culture, and wisely jettisoned the rest. There are numerous signs advertising "fabulous shirtings", and shops selling deerstalkers, pipe tobacco and badger-hair shaving brushes. The streets have names like Elgin Road and Old Court House Street, while the profusion of gentlemen's clubs is only rivalled by Pall Mall in London.

There was so much to do there that we delayed our onward journey to Baghdad by several days, giving us ample time to locate a suitable form of transport. One of our cultural excursions was a visit to Lady Gemima Thistlethwaite and Margaret Featherstonehaugh, the last remaining outpost of the Raj. Masaki's transformation before genuine aristocracy was astounding, his hair practically brushing the carpet when delivering an ornate bow. Masaki is the sort of manservant who only displays his true skills to those worthy of them. In the company of masters whom he considers second rate, such as ourselves, he simply can't be bothered.

The two ladies fussed over us, serving us an elaborate tea and demanding to hear all the gossip from London, such as the recent coronation celebrations and the effects of decimalisation on the price of gin. We asked them if they had any useful tips on transport systems to Iraq, but they had only ever left Calcutta by elephant. I saw a flicker of interest pass over Masaki's mask, and lo and behold, by the next morning he had managed to locate us an elephant and a team of porters for the journey to Baghdad.

The elephant, much like the Japanese manservant, is an inscrutable beast with laws all of its own. Fortunately for us, the two species differ in that the elephant needs to eat 600 pounds of green matter every day. This makes for a very slow and laborious journey, since Clive had to keep stopping to forage for tasty branches and leaves. A journey that should have taken us a few weeks ended up lasting for nearly three months.

However, the thought of reaching our final destination kept my mind focused during our crawling progress through India, Pakistan and Iran. We were heading towards the cradle of civilisation, to the fertile plains that once gave birth to Mesopotamia, the place where the Sumerian people devised our laws and invented literature, astronomy, mathematics and the word for alcohol. We were going towards the watery lands that bequeathed us the legend of Noah's Ark, a land where the gods created the first civilised men out of clay to serve them as slaves, and where walls forty feet thick enclosed a world of wickedness, pleasure and indulgence such as has never been equalled since. We were, in short, about to enter Babylon.

As visitors to modern-day Iraq, we appreciated Caliph Abu-al-Abbas's decision in 749 to transfer the seat of power from Damascus to Kufa, in what was then called Uruk. The resulting architecture was freed from the prosaic influence of Hellenism and replaced with a much grander, more mystical Persian Zoroastrianism. In spite of a few bullet holes here and some toppled statues of Saddam Hussein there, we could see that during its heyday Baghdad must have rivalled Constantinople for esoteric exuberance.

Victor, not really paying attention to my ramblings, only showed interest in the fact that the Sumerians had invented the word for alcohol. The glories of ancient Mesopotamia were not intoxicating enough for him, and we had to go on a tedious search for a non-existent tavern. My dipsomaniac chum soon discovered that one is as likely to find a bar serving alcohol in Baghdad as an opium den in Knightsbridge.

When we returned to our room at the Babylon Palace Hotel, we found that we had had a brush with the Thief of Baghdad. This was a great drawback, since over half of my winnings from the Thai Bride Sweepstake had been in my wallet. Masaki had the remainder and was quite keen to hang on to it, but I suggested trying to double it again by betting on something or other. The solution came when we switched on the television and saw an Arab reporter shouting at the cameras while some camels bounded along behind him.

Camel racing is one of the most singularly diverting sports I have ever come across. It combines all the thrills of the gee-gees, but with the added spectacle of these majestic creatures cantering along the sand track with a backdrop provided by the undulating dunes of the Syrian Desert. It also differs from British horse racing in that there are no boring rules and restrictions regarding the use of stimulants and tampering with the breeding process. Consequently the camels perform at the very best their species is capable of, and sometimes a little bit better.

After losing a few thousand Dinar on the first few races, to the palpable alarm of Victor and Masaki, I soon got the hang of it, and started backing winners. It was easy — one simply had to watch the camels that limped over to the starting gate then mysteriously jerked into action when their trainer shoved a syringe into their haunches.

We returned to the hotel with twice as much money as we had when we arrived in Baghdad, and I allowed Victor to squander some of it on some coveted souvenirs. He came back from the bazaar with a delightful prayer mat with an AK-47 embroidered on it and a compass indicating the direction of Mecca. I pointed out how useful that would be for the continuation of our journey to Addis Ababa, or at least it would be if we were travelling on the shoulders of a giant who could simply step over the Red Sea.

NIGHTLIFE:
FAT TARIQ'S BURKHA FOLLIES

TUCKED AWAY IN the city's eastern quarter, Fat Tariq's eccentric "Burkha Follies" is a night resort that most gentlemen visitors to Baghdad feel compelled to attend at least once during the course of their stay. Fat Tariq, a jovial cove of some 21 stones, is famed for always being in attendance to welcome his guests and to reign omnipotently over his harem of lithesome beauties with a firm but fair despotism. He is not your typical Iraqi, those who have spoken to him report that they can detect the merest trace of a Burnley accent, although he maintains adamantly that he was born in Basra and has never ventured further west than Ar-Rutba.

The unique selling point of Fat Tariq's establishment is that all his showgirls are ladies of impeccable breeding who remain in "purdah" throughout the course of their performance, not revealing an inch of flesh other than the merest glimpse of a hand or ankle, and avoiding eye contact with the lascivious customers. Strangely enough this seems to provoke the audience to a frenzied appreciation of the spectacular, causing them to clamber over one another, shouting "death to the infidel" and beseeching the dancers to conceal even more of their physiques.

Naturally no alcohol is allowed to be served on the premises, which is probably just as well, as the frenzied atmosphere already requires a 15 strong team of eunuch bouncers to ensure that things don't get out of hand.

If any of the customers do get a little too frisky, Fat Tariq has the miscreant transported to a "chill out" room in the basement where they are "calmed down" using a choice selection of cattle prods, piano wire and rubber truncheons.

MYTHS & LEGENDS:
THE EMPHYSEMIAN

THE POTENT FABLE of the beautiful and fragile bird of Emphysemia, Persia, occurs in Middle Eastern, Greek and Egyptian mythology, and dates back more than three millennia. The Emphysemian was said to survive solely on a diet of high tar cigarettes which it chain smoked whilst languidly reclining on a pile of plumped up cushions. Each morning the sun god would stop his chariot to listen to the bird as it sang a rapturous if rather husky melody.

The myth has it that only one Emphysemian exists at any one time. Every 500 years or so the bird would develop incurable lung cancer, and within seven days would keel over and crumble to dust in its large ash-tray shaped nest. From these ashes sprang forth a new and fully formed Emphysemian, which after clearing its throat would immediately light up and recommence the cycle of self-destruction and resurrection.

Africa

Addis Ababa, Ethiopia, 22nd July

Pouves & Peartree (Expeditionary Suppliers) Ltd will shortly be hearing from me expanding at length on a point of some delicacy. For many months now I have been meaning to write to them to express my grave disappointment with their hessian travel undergarments and a number of other requisites, which I was bamboozled into purchasing before my departure by Mr Peartree Junior, who painted a lurid picture of the multiple indignities of travel across Asia and Africa. This is how he persuaded me to purchase the Anti-Termite Gauze, the Leech Desiccation Powder and the Rectal Sand Snorkel. At no point did he point out that these articles should not be used in conjunction with riding a camel. Unfortunately I did, and now I find myself hobbling dans le style du crabe.

After our visit to the camel races Masaki's thought processes were ineluctably drawn to our dromedary friends as the ideal mode of transport for our transfer to Addis Ababa. However, the brutes in close up turned out to be a good deal less enchanting than depicted on the celluloid of the talented Mr Lean. A camel is a curmudgeonly beast, with the neck of an ostrich and the dentition of a Frenchman. I am incredulous that anyone in their right mind would consider riding them at all, but for a journey of 2000 miles ... and, heavens above, wearing that snorkel.

You will glean from this entry that we did at least finally gain the next destination on our itinerary. Writing this in the vestibule of the Addis Ababa Hilton, an extra dry Martini clasped firmly in hand, and in an idealised state of complete immobility, I can start to imagine that life might possibly be worth living once again.

By the time we embarked on our camel trek, the hardships Gustav and I had shared had eclipsed personal differences, and we plodded laboriously through the miles of endless sand grimly determined to grin and bear it. As we passed through Iraq and Jordan we were at least enchanted sporadically along the way by encounters with itinerant Bedouin herdsmen. Much to our surprise they were not only happy to offer us goats, sheep, daughters, camels and the like, but also seemed to be in possession of a great deal of interesting archaeological relics which they wished to sell. When questioned they suggested that most of it came from some minor Iraqi museum or other, which by some great good fortune was having "a bit of a clear out" at that time, with many artefacts going for a song.

I am glad to report that by the time we had reached Egypt the flow of ancient artefacts on offer did not abate, and if anything increased in quality and availability. One delightful fellow produced an old Gladstone bag from the folds of his garment and revealed from within some rather dainty trifles miraculously preserved from ancient Egypt. Gustav recoiled in horror at the sight of the mummified remains, but I have to say that the goods on offer particularly intrigued me. One carefully bandaged morsel purported to be the right hand of Amenhotep III, and on closer inspection there was revealed a manual appendage of some elegance. As a man accustomed to carrying a lucky rabbit's foot I thought that a pharaoh's hand, in all likelihood, might contain at least five times the magical qualities of its rodent counterpart. Five guineas secured the deal and I wedged it firmly between my hessian draws and liberty bodice in the hope it will draw good luck towards us on our ongoing journey.

Our ensuing journey across the parched lands of North Africa was an endless task of endurance, discomfort, thirst and unremitting boredom. It almost came as a relief on the third day of a sand storm, as the clouds of dust finally settled, to find ourselves confronted by armed Toureg brigands who waved guns in our faces (not for the first time on this trip) and demanded unfettered access to our luggage.

Gustav looked on in mute horror as our assailants riffled through his clothes cases, scuffing up his Lobb Oxfords and dancing about wearing his hand-stitched Egyptian cotton underpants on their heads. I am ashamed to admit that after the ennui of the previous days, I was faintly amused by this spectacle until, that is, they unearthed, horror of horrors, a pristine case of my vintage port. I am not a brave man, but to see the contents of a bottle of Borges Vintage 1970 being slowly poured onto the desert floor was surely more than any man could be expected to take. I involuntarily lunged forward. My initial instinct was to throw myself headlong onto the purply patch in the sand and attempt to strain the liquid residue through my teeth, but I lost my footing somewhat and found myself unexpectedly engaged in hand-to-hand combat with one of the brigands.

As we tusselled in a rather untidy manner, my newly acquired Egyptian artefact was dislodged from my waistband and lay exposed upon the sand. A screech of terror went up, followed by the general hubbub of Arabian babble. Extricating my head from the sand, I observed that our attackers were slowly backing away, jabbering as they went, staring fixedly in abject fear at Amenhotep III's withered digits. Surmising that they felt even more strongly than Gustav about my trinket, I picked up the hand and waved playfully in their direction. The result was instantaneous: an undignified scramble to remount their camels and a headlong dash for the horizon.

Although Gustav is reluctant to openly acknowledge the wisdom of my purchase, I can tell by his cheery disposition and his willingness to stand all the drinks now that we have reached Addis Ababa that bearing the "curse of the mummy" will be a small price to pay for the preservation of his wardrobe.

UNUSUAL TRIBES:
THE ANGORITE MONKS OF EGYPT

THE ANGORITE CULT of hermetic monasticism is said to have been founded by Saint Clovius of Egypt (288-361) who decided that he would throw off the yoke of the world on the grounds that everyday life was "tremendously vulgar, full of greed and dull as ditchwater". By the end of the fourth century AD there were several hundred angorite adherents living solitary lives of contemplation in caves or small huts dotted about the vast deserts of Egypt and Syria. An angorite's religious devotion was expressed through a life of extreme aestheticism, drawing abstract designs on the wall of his cave, and by a technique known as 'cosification of the flesh'. This was achieved by the wearing of simple garments made entirely out of angora wool, the idea being that the eradication of worldly discomforts would equip the monk to apply his mind more fully to the contemplation of the holy mysteries and God.

Philpott's

Ancient Curses and the 'Evil Eye'
(Abominatus ocularum)

Fig 297. Prophylactic measures against Abominatus ocularum

Whilst travelling through North Africa and especially Egypt you will find an impressive array of the curses and spells to sample. For example, by walking in the hallowed footsteps of the illustrious Howard Carter and plundering a pharaoh's tomb or two it is virtually guaranteed that a curse will be brought down upon your head. When you arrive back home in Pinner your neighbours will swoon with envy at your impressive rash of boils, and your social kudos will burgeon as recurring plagues of frogs and pestilence are visited upon your family for many generations to come.

Alternatively, experiment with provoking the evil eye. The merest cheeky glance at the wife of an Arab street vendor will stir him up to such paroxysms of rage that he will cast the eye upon you, resulting in the death of any goats you may own, withering of the fruit in your orchard, and, naturally, impotence.

UNUSUAL TRIBES:
THE MERBOYS OF THE NILE

THE HAZARDS OF travelling by dhow are manifold at the best of times, but the gentleman traveller will find it very difficult to maintain suitable standards of personal grooming during a trip down the Nile. After only a few days, if the constant pitching of the vessel hasn't messed up your parting beyond all recognition, then the bursts of river spray caused by passing speedboats soon will. It goes without saying that you will not find enough stability to correctly wax your moustache, and you will be in grave danger of arriving in Cairo for your appointment with the Vizier looking like a scarecrow that has been fished out of Niagara Falls.

But help is at hand. The merboys of the Nile always make their appearance during particularly rough weather. Recognisable by their high pitched wailing and their half-houseboy, half-fish bodies, they swim alongside passing dhows clutching mirrors, combs and razors. Simply lean your weathered visage over the side, and a willing merboy will trim your moustache, tidy up your hair and give you the closest shave you've ever had. The whole process only takes a few minutes, and you will be left looking like the cat's whiskers. The merboys have no use for money, but it is traditional to tip them with a sardine or two, or a lobster if you are particularly satisfied with the service.

UNUSUAL TRIBES:
THE STERLING DERVISHES OF EGYPT

IN AN ESOTERIC offshoot of the Moslem practice of circumcision of the male, an Egyptian cult has shifted the attention from the penis to the mouth. At the age of 13, male members of the Sterling Dervish have their upper lip stiffened.

The ritual takes place in a ceremonial tent especially erected for the occasion. The head dervish, or tasha, prepares the youth by placing about his person the ritual objects of a trilby, winceyette pyjamas, a monocle, a miniature whisky and soda and a whangee cigarette holder. He then instructs the youth in the higher ideals of the cult. This involves cigarette lighting technique, mixing Dry Martinis, instructions on playing baccarat and a tip for the 3.20 camel race in Cairo.

The tasha then performs the operation by injecting the youth's upper lip with a chemical compound very similar to Botox. This temporarily hardens the lip, keeping it stiff for about three months. The youth may ask for his lip to be re-stiffened at one-year intervals thereafter, should he feel he has strayed from the path of formality and upstanding behaviour.

Butembo, RD Congo, 12th August

I write this by the sputtering light of an oil lamp in the rather insalubrious surroundings of the campsite in the grounds of the Catholic Mission Guest House, Butembo, Democratic Republic of Congo. There was "no room at the inn", we were told by the desk clerk of the Guest House itself, with what I detected as a slight smirk. If the religious origins of the establishment are the object of such blasphemous ridicule by the staff, then perhaps they should consider changing its name. How about The Gloomy Concrete Bunker Full of Cockroaches Guest House?

This was a far cry from Ethiopia, where the facilities of the Addis Ababa Hilton had revived us from the rigours of camel travel. While luxuriating in the thermal bath in our suite, I had received a telephone call from Masaki, who insisted I join him at the former Grand Palace of Haile Selassie, now a museum. What he wanted to show me, apart from some splendid photographs of the Emperor presenting George V with a pride of Abyssinian lions in 1924, was Haile Selassie's sedan chair. It was a glorious item carved out of a solid piece of mahogany, with exquisite carvings on the sides depicting the history of the Lions of Judah, ornamental gold filigree on the canopy and a pair of seats upholstered in purple velvet.

"Ideal vehicle for next journey," Masaki whispered to me out of earshot of the museum guard. "First-class idea, old thing," I hissed back, "but how the devil do you propose we remove it?"

"The winged serpent cannot bite his pilot," he replied. I had learnt by then that the more abstruse Masaki's aphorisms, the more sophisticated his plans, so I merely nodded sagely while he went to have a word with the guard.

Sure enough, at eleven o'clock that night, just as Victor and I were enjoying a nightcap in the Africa Bar of the hotel, Masaki enjoined us to follow him out of the hotel. The inscrutable one had packed all our luggage and settled our bill, and all we had to do was

enter the taxicab that awaited us outside. We were
driven to the Grand Palace museum and there beheld a
curious sight. Haile Selassie's sedan chair was sitting
on the pavement outside, the gold trim glinting in the
moonlight. At each of the four carrying posts there was
a tall, athletic Ethiopian with a determined, noble look
about him. Masaki explained that the four men, in
training for the forthcoming Commonwealth Games, would
be replaced with similar fellows at various points
between Addis Ababa and our destination, Butembo.

Each evening we camped wherever we happened to be when
the first of the bearers collapsed. The bearers would
light a campfire and cook us a meal of roast Thomson's
gazelle (delicious with pan-fried tsetse flies and a
salad of paw-paw leaves).

As we entered the Rift Valley the terrain became swampy
and more hazardous, but our new set of Ugandan shot
putters were up to the task. Conditions inside the sedan
chair became more and more uncomfortable as we neared
the fringes of the Congo jungle, and each of us dealt
with the intolerable heat in his own way. Victor
fashioned a curious form of burkah out of towels, while
Masaki used origami techniques to create a dainty little
fan out of a banana tree leaf. I was already wearing an
ultra-lightweight linen safari suit from Gieves &
Hawkes, and I draped the windows of the sedan chair with
crepe-de-chine and linen to block out the sun.

Once we had crossed the border into the Congo at
Kasindi, we found ourselves in the thick jungle of the
Virunga National Park. According to our map, the
settlement of Butembo was only a few miles further.
Waves of relief were just beginning to wash over us when
there was a sudden commotion in the trees. Monkeys
screeched, parrots fluttered and the leaves seemed to be
shaking as if in a thunderstorm. Too scared to peer out
of our Turnbull & Asser canopy, we only heard the
terrified screams of our bearers and the sound of their
footsteps as they scurried away. Then there was silence.

Or rather the backdrop of creaking, crackling,
twittering and shuddering that passes for silence in the
jungle. Then, as if nothing had happened, the sedan

chair was hoisted up and we continued our journey.

After many more hours, a glance at Trubshawe indicated that we must be nearing our destination. I pulled back the window coverings to communicate with the bearers – and hastily pulled them closed again.

"My God, we're really in it now, gents," I hissed to the other two.

"Whatever is the matter?" said Victor, "your face has gone completely albino."

"Shh! For God's sake be quiet! Masaki, do me a great favour and put your head carefully through the curtains, and tell me there are not a pair of gorillas carrying us to Kingdom Come."

Masaki obliged, and regretfully informed me that this was indeed the case. I flicked through Trubshawe for help. In a brief, somewhat dismissive passage, he referred to gorillas as "only threatening if one tries to enter their territory. They may also occasionally try to steal human items for decorative use in their tree homes." That explained it. Unaware of our presence, these apes had picked up our sedan chair when the bearers ran off, and were taking it to their dwelling to use as a sofa or a climbing frame, or simply to smash it up for fun. Unless we bailed out before they got there, we would suffer a similar fate.

I instructed Masaki to repack all our clothes and prepare to abandon ship. He hauled out the suitcases, hatboxes and travelling trunks first, and then one by one Victor, Masaki and myself leapt out of the sedan chair into the undergrowth. We walked and walked for several hours with visions of comfortable beds, mosquito nets and gin fizzes. In the end we had to make do with a tent on a patch of grass and some dirty water.

Victor Agamemnon Darkwood Esq.

Suite 17, The Sheridan Club, St. James's, London SW1

Kofi Annan,
Secretary-General of the United Nations
United Nations Building
New York, New York, 10017, USA

The Grounds of the
Catholic Mission Guest House,
Butembo,
Democratic Republic of Congo.

13th August

Dear Mr Annan,

Gustav Temple, my travel companion, and I are currently engaged in a rather singular jaunt about the globe, engaged upon a mission of international importance, namely a crusade to spread cordiality and gentlemanly standards of behaviour around the world.

We realise that you are a tremendously busy cove, up to your ears with all sorts of peace keeping activities, but in the light of our important work, we had hoped you might find a little time to help us out of our current predicament (beset by insects and all manner of beastliness) by sending some UN troops (a couple of burly fellows in a Challenger tank would probably do the trick) to extricate us from the jungle.

We are cognisant of the fact that getting help to us may take a little time, so if I might be so bold, could I also request another small favour, I was wondering if you could possibly have a hamper (our usual suppliers are Johnstone and Triblet Ltd, St. James, London – I'm sure you'll find their number in the book) dispatched to us at the above address, just to keep our spirits up until the search party arrives. I'll leave the selection to Mr Johnstone, who always knows what I like, but it may be worth reminding him to include a large jar of Thedgleley's Chunky-Cut "Olde Tyme" Marmalade as we are bang out of it at the moment.

Thanking you for your kind help in advance.

Cordial regards

Vic Darkwood

United Nations, New York, NY 10017, U.S.A.

27th August

Dear Mr Darkwood,

Mr Annan has asked me to thank you on his behalf for your recent letter.

Although we are sorry to hear about your present plight, we regret to inform you that it is not the role of the UN to organise individual rescues based on perceived danger from "insects" or general "beastliness".

We suggest you may wish to contact the British Council or Unesco, who would be better qualified to advise you regarding the advisability of undertaking "cultural work" in the Congo in the present political climate.

Yours sincerely

Terrence Bunyan,
On behalf of Kofi Annan,
Secretary-General of the United Nations

CONGO
The Herald

Missing Journo Found Serving Afternoon Tea

RD CONGO: A BRITISH JOURNALIST, MISSING FOR SEVEN MONTHS AND PRESUMED DEAD, HAS BEEN FOUND WORKING AT A GENTLEMAN'S CLUB IN THE CONGO JUNGLE. TONY NBEKO REPORTS

LAST MAY NIGEL BUTTERWORTH, Africa correspondent for Britain's Daily Mail, suddenly disappeared while researching an article on gorilla sanctuaries. At the time it was presumed that Congolese rebels had kidnapped him, but no request for a ransom ever arrived.

This Tuesday, a group of Sudanese businessmen travelling through the Congo jungle were offered refreshments by some jovial Matusi tribesmen. They were taken into a small hut, which from the outside looked like any other simple adobe dwelling in this part of the jungle. But inside, the hut had been adapted into a convincing replica of a typical English gentleman's club, complete with liveried manservant.

The inside walls had been panelled with a special mud closely resembling the colour of oak; crushed berries and vegetables arranged in swirling patterns on the floor approximated an Axminster rug; and a collection of glass beads, Coca-cola bottles and fireflies arranged on the ceiling became an ersatz chandelier.

The founders of 'Churchill's Club', as

Tunji Bodewale relaxing in the smoking room of Churchill's Club

it is named, Ade Bombasa and Tunji Bodewale, explained that none of the typical local refreshment facilities appealed to them. "We don't like to sit on the floor surrounded by insects, while a fat woman serves us gruel in a leaf. We read a book about the Pall Mall clubs in London and decided that we needed something similar here in the Congo."

The attention to detail is stunning, considering the founders only had a handful of badly reproduced photographs as reference. The furniture,

made from buffed rhinoceros hide, is in the Queen Anne style, and tea is served at precisely four o'clock every day. But the real coup de grace is the presence of "Old Hawkins", as Nigel Butterworth has been christened by the 27 members. With constant cries of "Come on old chap, top up my glass!" and "Get a move on with those kippers, Hawkins!", the poor fellow is kept on his toes for most of the day. His outfit is an amusing rendition of a butler's uniform that allows for the soaring humidity of the jungle. A black loincloth has been fitted with coat-tails, and around his neck is a bow tie fashioned from ostrich feathers.

Although his employers at the Daily Mail are desperate to have Butterworth returned home, the local authorities are reluctant to intervene. They claim that though the journalist has been officially kidnapped, he is being kept in conditions far more civilised than might have been expected, and is providing a much-needed boost to morale among the politically marginalized Matusi tribespeople.

COUP DE HAT

★ ★ ★ ★ ★ ★ ★ ★

REVOLUTIONARY MILLINERS

ARE YOU A DISILLUSIONED MILITARY LEADER WITH AN EYE ON THE BIG TIME?

DO YOU ASPIRE TO BE THE BADDEST TIN POT DICTATOR SINCE HISTORY BEGAN?

WELL, IF YOU WANT BE THE HEAD, GET A HAT.

NO RUTHLESS DESPOT IN THE MAKING WOULD BE SEEN DEAD EMBARKING UPON A COUP D'ÉTAT WITHOUT THE APPROPRIATE HEADGEAR. COUP DE HAT CAN SUPPLY ALL YOUR MILLINERY NEEDS, FROM YOUR FIRST PHOTO OPPORTUNITY FIRING YOUR PISTOL AS YOU STORM THE PRESIDENTIAL PALACE TO THE MORE SEDATE REVIEWING OF YOUR TROOPS AFTER THE HUBBUB HAS DIED DOWN. BE SUITABLY ATTIRED FOR THAT TRICKY INITIAL TV BROADCAST OR CHOOSE HEADGEAR THAT WILL MAINTAIN YOUR DIGNITY WHEN BEING SNUBBED BY FOREIGN DIPLOMATS. JUST REMEMBER, LOOK GOOD WHILE IT LASTS. WITH CAREFUL USE YOUR HAT MAY WELL OUTLIVE YOUR STINT IN THE TOP JOB.

COUP DE HAT
PO BOX 18804
KAMPALA
UGANDA.

COCKTAILS
HOW TO MIX THEM

THE MASAI MARTINI

The Masai Martini is best enjoyed at a height of 600 metres, ideally in a balloon, where the blood content oxidises and gives the gin some extra "bite". The recipe was created in 1972 by Masai herdsmen. These nomadic tribespeople, whose sole resource is their cattle, survive during arduous journeys across the veldt by making small incisions in the leg of a bullock and draining off some of its blood to drink. This protein-rich snack is usually their only form of sustenance for weeks at a time. The Masai Martini is a by-product of this ingenious nutritional innovation, and is used by the Masai to celebrate the completion of a business transaction.

THE RECIPE:

4 parts cattle blood
(preferably bullock)

3 parts vodka
1 part Vermouth
1 sheep's eyeball to garnish

NB: In some cases the last two ingredients are omitted, making this cocktail, strictly speaking, a Bloody Mary.

BY

' ROBERT '

OF THE AMERICAN BAR,
CASINO MUNICIPAL, NICE,
AND LATE OF THE
EMBASSY CLUB, LONDON

Cape Town, South Africa, 30th August

I write this, having briefly caught up with the fleeting chimera of civilised living in the Admiralty Bar of the Hyatt Cape Town.

Back in Butembo, it had seemed very likely that we had come to the end of the road. Perishing ignobly, devoured by soldier ant and tsetse fly under a piece of threadbare canvas in the Congolese jungle, was not precisely how I had envisaged my ideal demise. (I had at least hoped for a few specially employed "wailing women" and limitless bunches of lilies.) Masaki had succumbed to an accumulated dose of toxins from the numerous insect bites he had sustained along the way, and now lay in a delirious fever, the Mission informed us that no rooms would be available for the next five weeks and the likelihood of locating ongoing transport seemed almost nil.

By the fourth night Masaki was ranting in the most alarming manner and the disconcerting sounds of the forest seemed to be closing in on us. Just then a rapid scratching sound came from the front flap of our tent and through the canvas we could see the flickering of a flame. Gustav and I, not known for our bravery, scampered back into the far recesses of the tent and did our best to use Masaki on his sick bed as a human shield.

The tent flap was torn open and there stood a curious pygmy barely four and a half foot tall holding a flaming torch.

"Come," he intoned in a basso profundo that seemed incongruous with his diminutive stature.

Having no better options, we gingerly stepped out of the tent and were swiftly led through the byways of Butembo until we came to a small hut with a corrugated iron roof. We were ushered inside into a small room lined by bookcases and furnished at the far end by a large oak desk piled high with various tomes, files and papers. Behind this wall of stationery and just visible above it we could make out a shock of white hair through a large pall of tobacco smoke.

"They come," announced our guide in the same theatrically deep timbre.

Almost like the parting of the Red Sea the wall of books was breeched and there rose from a seat a fellow not dissimilar from Moses himself (although as far as I can recall Moses has never been depicted smoking a Calabash and wearing horn-rimmed spectacles).

"Mr Temple and Mr Darkwood, let me welcome you to my little hovel. I trust Derek has treated you well?" He gestured towards his pygmy manservant and then glanced down at the bottle I was carrying. "Good God, what a sight for sore eyes. Any chance of a snifter of that there Ardbeg?" The ice was immediately broken.

It soon transpired that our host was a medical man, Angus McPhail, who had once held a senior role with the Mission, but had decided on early retirement to free up more time to pursue his joint hobbies of reading, drinking and morphine addiction. He miraculously seemed to know all about us: our expedition, our lack of accommodation and our urgent need for onward transport.

We spent a jolly evening. First we finished off the Ardbeg, and then sent Angus's manservant together with a band of pygmy porters back to our camp to fetch a case of rare single malts. On their return they expressed concern that Masaki seemed to be rapidly catching on as the premiere dining spot for all the local mosquitoes, so our host suggested that they also retrieved our trusty servant and the luggage, and that he would be delighted if we would do him the honour of staying with him for a day or two.

By the end of the evening we had not only managed to rid ourselves of our sobriety, but had also solved our on-going transport difficulties. It seems that Angus owned an ancient hot air balloon, which he had kept in storage in a shed at the back. With the help of the pygmies he insisted that he would have us embarking on our forward journey "in no time at all" and that with a bit of luck with the prevailing winds we could expect to arrive on the west coast of Africa "within days".

When we did leave, the whole of Butembo turned out to see us off. I decided to wear my old uniform once again to give the impression that we were fellows who knew exactly what they were up to. It took us less than ten minutes to realise that we hadn't a clue.

As it turned out Angus's optimistic appraisal of our flight time was hopelessly ill-calculated. The prevailing wind had taken it into its head to blow from north to south, and we therefore bypassed all the convenient ports such as Ponte-Noire and Luanda, and instead drifted steadily south, passing over Angola and Namibia. It was only after a couple of weeks that we awoke one morning to discover ourselves drifting above Cape Town. Considering that in overshooting this destination we would be lost forever over the vast expanses of the Atlantic, we decided it might be wise to make the swiftest of swift descents. Rather rashly in my opinion, instead of toying with the valve release mechanism, Gustav impulsively scrambled up the side of the basket and started slashing at the balloon with his swordstick. I'm not sure exactly how many skyscrapers we bumped into on the way down. All I do know is that by the time our basket lodged itself on the top of the Hyatt Cape Town we had lost several items of our luggage over the side and we were all in an advanced state of concussion and shock. It was only after the emergency services had retrieved us from the roof that we became aware that one of our lost cases contained the remainder of our cash. We were once again going to have to indulge in some quick thinking if we were to have an earthly chance of getting to South America.

Vic Darwin

NATURAL HISTORY:
THE HANDLEBAR GAZELLE

WHEN VISITING SOUTH AFRICA it is customary to go on at least one of the many safaris on offer in order to satisfy one's curiosity as to the strange beasts that lurk beyond the confines of the city. One natural curiosity that is well worth tracking down is the Handlebar Gazelle, a fine beast roughly 6 feet in height and blessed through some quirk of nature with impressive sub-nasal growth that strongly resembles a gentleman's handlebar moustache. Zoologists differ in their theories as to why evolution should have led to such a development in the animal, but most are agreed that during the mating season females seem to favour those males with the more imposing moustache growth. It therefore seems reasonable to assume that, similar to human beings, the sporting of a nicely turned moustache is a clear indication of a male's health and virility.

ART & CULTURE:
MUSEUM OF UNUSUAL PETS

IF ONE IS to voyage through southern Africa, one simply cannot afford to miss this charming museum. The stuffed exhibits date back to the 19th century, the most ancient being Prince Pückler-Muskau's chameleon, which this eccentric German traveller trained to crawl about his pipe in 1875. Ernest Hemingway, though principally interested in the killing of animals, was particularly fond of a pet baboon named Wilbert, without whom he never left his tent. Visitors to the museum will find it difficult to avoid Wilbert's stately gaze from his glass vitrine in the Great Apes section. But while most of the species on show have their origins in the Dark Continent, some have been imported from other areas. Lady Ottoline Morel's ocelot, for example, originally hailed from the Americas. The Astor family were kind enough to donate the stuffed ghekko which, when alive, enjoyed all the privileges of upper class accommodation in the family mansion at Hever, with its own suite of inter-connecting cages commanding fine views over the Kent countryside.

THE MUSEUM OF UNUSUAL PETS
12 Township Approach, Cape Town

PARLONS PIDGIN!

VARIOUS FORMS OF Pidgin English are spoken all over Africa, the most common being Nigerian Pidgin. Here is a sample of some useful phrases that will undoubtedly endear you to the locals.

Ol' boy, why you dey show ma fefe – you is not man of timber and calibre.
I say, old bean, why the airs and graces? I can see from your shabby attire that you're not a true gentleman.

See am as e siddon. No face! Everywhere tinted!
Observe that cove seated yonder. He looks surprisingly unhappy for someone with such a splendid pair of sun-resistant spectacles.

Abeg giam!
This pointless discussion on the relative merits of two soccer teams, neither of whom interest me in the slightest, seems likely to result in fisticuffs.

As man land, man eye brush vest. Man begin knack tori.
Descending the staircase, a rather fetchingly dressed young lady caught my eye. I approached her and wooed her with a dazzling series of bons mots.

Sontin dey do you sokoto trousa. Soup wey sweet na money kill am.
There is a major flaw in the design of your traditional trousers. Surely you understand that good things cost money?

Sidon there now wit shakeez in slipas, sidon look na dog name.
You cut a rather louche figure, sitting on your porch drinking wine all day in a pair of slippers.

Pouves &
Peartree

Since 1714

For those new to the colonies, the insufferable heat of Africa can send one's head into quite a spin. Thoughts will inevitably become muddled and analytical faculties will be severely impaired, but now with the Pouves and Peartree's Head Refrigerator you can keep a cool head on your shoulders at all times and reap multiple benefits as a result.

Pouves & Peartree's
HEAD REFRIGERATOR

Compact and discreet, the handy back-mounted refrigeration unit and plexiglass 'micro-climate' hood will keep your thoughts clear for social events, tricky business meetings or unpleasant encounters with overly-pushy street vendors. Whilst those around you faint from heat exhaustion, you will be able to clinch that vital deal or woo that special lady unencumbered by the worst excesses of a filthy foreign climate. And rest assured, at all times, an oval frontal aperture ensures easy access for pipe-smoking, canapés and witty conversation.

The Americas

Belem, Brazil, 14th September

Our prospects in Cape Town did not look very good. We had nowhere to sleep and our collective coffers amounted to £12.74. Masaki suggested stocking up on bananas and bread to keep us going for as long as possible. Victor was all for buying several bottles of cheap Scotch for the same purpose. I had a much better idea. "Gentlemen, if we are imminently to join the serried ranks of the poor, then we may as well bow out with dignity." We repaired to the Admiralty Bar of the Hyatt Cape Town, where Victor ordered a round of Dry Martinis and a glass of green tea for Masaki. I for my part had some sartorial matters of some urgency to attend to.

I had seven pairs of brogues that needed polishing, eighteen Sea Island cotton shirts ready for laundering and a dinner jacket in need of a good overhaul, after months of languishing in a suitcase. I popped upstairs to the sixth floor of the hotel and deposited the shoes outside a room with a 'Do not disturb' sign on the door, knowing they would be taken away and cleaned and returned to the same spot the following morning. I loitered about in the corridor until a chambermaid came along with her trolley. "I say there," I said, "your colleague seems to have forgotten to take my jacket and shirts. I wonder if you'd mind awfully …?" She promised to leave them on a hanger outside the door the next morning, so as not to disturb my sleeping wife, who was suffering from a touch of influenza.

When I rejoined the other two, Victor was thumbing through a copy of the *Cape Town Enquirer*, having run out of things to say to Masaki after the first aphorism of the day. "By jove, this looks rum," he said, pointing at a large advertisement. *Crew members wanted urgently. HMS Longfellow sails Monday 7th September at midday. Applicants should report to the Harbourmaster's Office before 8pm on Sunday 31st August.*

"Current time and date, please, Masaki?" I asked the inscrutable one.

"Five pm, Sunday 31st August, Master," was his reply.

"I suggest we finish our drinks at leisure and then saunter down to see the Harbourmaster."

The Harbourmaster informed us that HMS Longfellow did indeed require more crew members, without which she would be unable to embark on a two-week cruise to Brazil carrying several hundred British passengers. Consequently, Captain James Peabody was not in a position to be too picky. "Between you and me," confided the Harbourmaster, "he'd take you on if you had never set foot on a ship in your life." Victor and I exchanged glances and said nothing.

Thus it was that myself, Victor and Masaki were hired on the spot to fill the posts of croupier, wine waiter and cabin boy respectively. Once installed in our cabin, we were shown to our positions and our tasks were explained to us. One might assume that we had landed on our feet, in a sense, what with being assigned duties that reflected our interests, but sadly this was not to be the case.

The ship casino was one of those terribly vulgar establishments that one is occasionally forced to visit in resorts such as Blackpool or Las Vegas. The games of roulette were played amid a nauseating cocktail consisting of one part piped muzak, two parts clanking one-armed bandit and six parts cheap perfume of perma-tanned hoi polloi from the Home Counties, none of whom ever gambled more than five dollars at a time.

Victor's fate was equally ignominious. Having assumed he'd be given the keys to the cellar, he smugly assumed that he would be the drunkest person in the dining room. But he found out that the snooty maitre d' was the sole warden of the wine cellar. Every night Victor would return to the cabin with his apron covered in wine stains and a stony faced look, which indicated the stains were the result of shaking hands when serving other people with wine. "Any luck?" I would ask. "No. I knocked back what I thought was a glass of gin someone had left on a table, but it turned out to be water. Ugh!"

However, compared to Masaki, Victor and I were having an easy life. Captain Peabody had taken a bit of a shine to his new cabin boy and made no attempt to disguise it. "Ah, there you are, Shanghai Lil," would boom the Captain's baritone as he burst into our cabin at odd hours, such as three in the morning. "Time to scrub the poop deck, boy! No need to dress, come as you are, left, right, left, right!" This most gentlemanly of gentlemen's gentlemen would spend the next hour or two hunched over mop and pail, while the Captain bellowed out anecdotes about his high jinks on the South China Seas, the loose folds of his silk dressing gown flapping in the wind.

Our off-duty hours were not much more pleasant, due to the poor quality of the passengers. We roamed the decks in search of the eccentric Indian or the Italian countess portrayed in seafaring novels and films, but the quest was a futile one. The only incident of any note was when Victor, having finally managed to pilfer some bottles of Liebfraumilch, slipped over on the quoits board during a game between some old ladies. Landing in the middle of the board and sending all the pieces flying, he said jocularly from his recumbent position: "Quoitus interruptus!" It was a splendid bon mot, I thought, but the unsophisticated passengers did not share my view.

When we finally caught sight of the dry land of South America, we were the first crew members in the queue to collect our wages. Victor had £14.50 deducted for the stolen Liebfraumilch and Masaki received an enormous tip from Captain Peabody. The minute the gangway was lowered, the three of us tripped down it with our luggage, and merged with the crowds in downtown Belem, eager to put the whole sorry business of paid employment behind us.

Parasites:
The Antimacassar worm
(Lumbricus macassarus soporificum)

Travellers to the Amazon may sometimes bring home more than they bargain for. A gentleman who inadvisably chooses to micturate off piste, for example, will probably find his urinary flow turned into a convenient conduit for all sorts of virulent parasites. We would suggest that the discerning diseasophile, for preference, should woo the Antimacassar Worm, as it is not only socially amusing, but can perform a serious social function.

Invaded by said worm the sufferer will show no ill-effects for up to 12 years, but one idle Christmas afternoon he will find the ligaments that attach the back of his skull to the spine suddenly gnawed away and the head will involuntarily slump forward onto the chest in a most hilarious manner. This will provide hearty laughter for all, but more importantly, the daintily woven chintz of the upholstery will be saved from the detrimental effects of corrosive macassar hair oil.

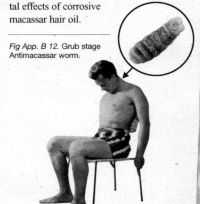

Fig App. B 12. Grub stage Antimacassar worm.

Pouves & Peartree

SAVIOURS OF SMOKING MATERIALS THE WORLD OVER

Peartree

Since 1714

Pouves & Peartree's
PIPE DINGHY

It's common knowledge that ocean-going liners often have the misfortune of colliding with icebergs and sinking without trace. In such circumstances, life boats have the nasty habit of becoming rapidly over-subscribed with women and screeching children, but now with the Pouves and Peartree Pipe Dinghy you can at least ensure that your pipe smoking activities remain uninterrupted by your impending appointment with the briny. As the poop deck is deluged, the Pipe Dinghy leaves your tobacco dry and your arms free for those essential swimming movements. 3 guineas (Nylon wrist leash supplied).

QUALITÉ SUPÉRIEURE

TOP DRAWER!

THE CAPTAIN REQUESTS THE PLEASURE
OF YOUR COMPANY

R.S.V.P.

THE INTERNATIONAL DATELINE

An integral part of any voyage across the Atlantic is
the crossing of the International Dateline.
It has always been the custom of HMS Longfellow
to allow our newest crew members to create their own
special celebrations for this occasion. On this voyage
we are pleased to announce that Mr Gustav Temple
(croupier), Mr Vic Darkwood (wine waiter) and
Mr Masaki Nakatake (cabin boy) will be in charge of
the proceedings, which will take place at
3pm on Saturday 12th July.
They have named their celebration 'Waves of Panache',
and judging by some of the outfits they have made,
it promises to be a highly diverting spectacle!

CUSTOMS & TRADITIONS:
BEACHCOMBING

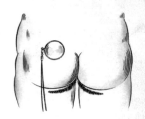

HAVING A 'BRAZILIAN' usually entails a very uncomfortable process for the ladies, involving strips of wax-covered paper being ripped off one's private parts. The sun-worshipping Brazilian gentlemen, too, have taken to wearing skimpy thongs to display their smooth, hairless skin, popularising the horrific phrase 'back, crack and sack' in their quest for depilatory one-upmanship. In a racy new development of this traditional gender rivalry between Rio de Janeiro's beautiful people, the gents seem currently to have the upper hand. Instead of depilating their entire backs or buttocks, they have taken to leaving areas of hair on their behinds to depict curious designs.

The most popular design is the Terry-Thomas, where a circle of hair to represent a monocle is left on one buttock, while a thin band of hair adorns the lower buttocks in the form of a pencil moustache. Other designs one can see parading about the Rio beaches are the Ken Dodd, the Jimmy Edwards and the Dennis Healey.

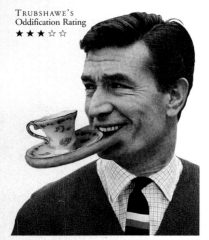

TRUBSHAWE'S
Oddification Rating
★ ★ ★ ☆ ☆

BODY ODDIFICATION
The Lip Saucer

INSPIRED BY THE antics of the Kayapo Indians who live along the upper tributaries of the Xingu River in Brazil, this daring cove has trained his lower lip into a handy teacup holding device. This allows him to attend garden parties and summer fetes without suffering from the age old awkwardness of attemping to hold a cup of tea, carry a plate of lightly buttered scones and shake the hand of the vicar, all at the same time.

Experienced 'lip saucerers' of an exhibitionist bent have been known to delight all and sundry at such events with a spot of hands-free Oolong consumption.

Iquitos, Peru, 9th October

I have unfortunately been obliged to sell one of my kidneys. I am currently rehabilitating in the cosy confines of the large wicker chair in the cocktail bar of the Amazonas Hotel, having decided (against medical advice) to increase the efficiency of my remaining organ by putting it through its paces.

The drama started to unfold shortly after our arrival in Belem, where we undertook a review of our coffers and found them sadly depleted. On stepping ashore, I had immediately invested some of the cash I had earned in a couple of crates of champagne. Similarly, Gustav gave vent to his frustrated lust for the gaming tables by immediately disappearing into some squalid dockside casino. Masaki, on the other hand, had prudently stashed away his lucre, so Gustav and I at least felt secure that we would have a few spondulicks in reserve if push came to shove. It was only when we had squandered a good percentage of our funds that Masaki dropped a bombshell by reminding us that one of the rules of our wager was that, although he was allowed to provide us with his services, he was only permitted to employ his own funds for personal use and could not make them available to finance travel expenses.

Once Gustav and I had calculated our remaining balance it came to no more than a few hundred pounds. Not a princely sum for the continuation of our journey. Mortified and angry, Gustav sulkily shoved a wad of cash into

Masaki's hand and ordered him to "at least make himself a little useful" and go in search of transport for the next leg of our trip.

On reflection it was probably not a good move to hector Masaki prior to one of his reconnaissance missions. It would only spur him on to further manifestations of inscrutable revenge, and indeed it did.

When he returned Masaki announced with something akin to triumph in his voice that we would be taking a "little trip in a boat". It soon turned out that what he meant by this was not the splendid steam ship from the film *Fitzcarraldo* that I had hoped for, but instead a thirty-foot hollowed-out tree trunk powered by six burley Amazonian Indians.

Masaki had only just fully recovered from his ill health in Africa and now it was Gustav's turn to fall foul of infirmity. He awoke after an afternoon snooze to find a large snake up one of his trouser legs and before he could extricate the beast it had sunk in its fangs and deposited their venom into Gustav's calf muscle. The reassurance from our Amazonian companions that the poison would not prove fatal did little to placate my travel companion.

Within a few hours Gustav's lower limb had become hugely swollen and he looked down at it with some alarm as he lay in the aft of the boat.

"Oh God, I think I'm in grave danger of losing the whole leg," he said, looking askance at Masaki.

"Mr Gustav, the Amazonians say the swelling will go down in eight hours," replied Masaki solicitously.

"Not my leg, you Nipponese nincompoop, the trouser leg. If this thing gets any larger my trousers will be ruined forever. Prepare for surgery," announced Gustav imperiously.

Masaki was sent scurrying in search of scissors, magnifying glass, pocket torch, and needle and thread. Then, instructed by Gustav, he set to work carefully unpicking the fine stitching along the inside leg. It was an arduous task. Gustav's tailor Mr Saxby prided himself on the invisibility and finesse of his needlecraft. With stitching this fine, one slip and the fraying could be terminal. After two hours Masaki had accomplished his operation with aplomb. The leg was saved and after several hours, when the swelling had subsided, Masaki was able to tread in Mr Saxby's hallowed footsteps, restitching the breeches as if they had never been tampered with in the first place.

And so to Iquitos, "Peru's Gateway to the Amazon". By the time we had reached this city in the heart of the Peruvian jungle Gustav was feeling a lot better but still slightly weakened by his ordeal. We had spent all of our remaining money on employing our boatmen and buying the provisions for the journey, and I don't mind admitting that I was getting to the end of my tether. We hadn't really had a pleasant time of it since leaving Addis Ababa and I'd be damned if we were going to accept some iniquitous and humiliating mode of conveyance for the onward journey. Rather optimistically I announced to my travel companions that this time it was my turn to 'bring home the bacon' and that I intended to go out into the town and not return until I had furnished our treasury with some serious amounts of coinage.

After several hours of wandering about town I had almost given up hope. I went into a telephone box in a last ditch attempt to track down in the phone book any establishment that looked vaguely likely to stage unofficial gaming. It was then that I saw it. A small sticker on the kiosk wall announced in Spanish and English, "Need ready cash? We pay top prices for your internal organs." Within the hour I was in pre-op.

Before the operation I nominated the left kidney as the one that I wished to sell. I have to admit it has been of precious little use to me over the last few years, aching horribly every time I give it work to do, and £12,000 seemed to be a particularly good price as I have a shrewd suspicion that it gave up functioning some time ago. In fact ever since the morbid piece of offal was removed I feel a lot better than I did when it was actually in situ. Quite naturally I gave the surgeon a false name and address when I signed the contract, just in case it happened to include a money back guarantee.

Noticias
Latin America

BRAZIL'S PURLEY KING

MANAUS, 27TH SEPTEMBER

A European man has been discovered reigning over a tribe of indigenous tribespeople in the remote Brazilian jungle. Joao Cardigoso reports.

Simon Fribbe, a former IT manager from Purley, England, is the self-proclaimed king of Fribland, an empire which extends as far as the village of Tapano in the north of the Mato grosso region. The Xingu Indians, always known for their excessive courtesy and pleasant nature, in contrast with most other tribes in this region, were happy to allow Mr Fribbe (or El Fribbo, as he is now known) to take over as their king.

Until Mr Fribbe's arrival, the Xingu people had enjoyed a primitive form of democratic socialism for over 4,000 years, having been untouched by the corrupting forces of Western civilisation. But when Mr Fribbe came along and offered to reign over them in the style of a British monarch, they readily consented, "Just for a change, really," as one of

the village elders put it.

Two years ago, Mr Fribbe had been travelling across Brazil on a morale-boosting exercise organised by his Purley-based firm, ProTech. During a jungle survival exercise he wandered off on his own, armed with nothing except two Kit-Kats and a thermos flask of instant coffee.

Mr Fribbe had been presumed dead by his firm until news broke of the discovery of the kingdom of Fribland, which had the distinct feel of one of the hilarious "skits" that the IT manager would perform at ProTech's annual Christmas party.

Fribland is run on very tight principles. Its supreme ruler, His Royal Highness King Fribbe I, has the ultimate mandate on all matters of internal affairs, finance and foreign policy. A stickler for punctuality, King Fribbe has made a complete overhaul of the community's transport system. During the period now known as BF (Before Fribbe), the villagers would drift about on the tributaries of the Amazon in dugout kayaks, arriving with slain animals and other supplies

A Fribonian Indian applies pinstripe-coloured woad to a friend's back

according to the whim of the tides. But now King Fribbe has devised a timetable for all kayaks, with precise times given for connecting services and severe penalties for unpunctual oarsmen. King Fribbe has respected the Xingu tradition of not wearing clothes, but insists that all citizens decorate their bodies with woad, painted on to resemble smart-casual clothing. King Fribbe now plans to make a bid for Fribland to host the 2012 Olympics.

COCKTAILS
HOW TO MIX THEM

THE MASTICATED MARTINI

In the wilds of the Peruvian jungle, where even the Amazon dares not meander, there dwells a tribe of Indians known as the Awaka. Theirs is a simple society based in adobe dwellings, with a language that does not have a word for 'lavatory'. However, when it comes to cocktails, the Awaka are head and shoulders above many so-called civilised European countries.

The Awaka womenfolk scour the jungle in search of certain rare herbs which, when chewed for several hours, closely resemble a very good Vermouth. Once masticated to a pulp, assisted by the natural enzymes released by the saliva, the Vermouth-flavoured pulp is spat into a wooden vessel and the liquid strained off. This is then shaken with gin and served in tall wooden goblets with a sliver of lemon rind.

THE RECIPE:

**2 parts jungle herbs
(masticated for 3 hours)**

**5 parts Plymouth gin
1 sliver lemon rind to garnish**

BY
'ROBERT'
OF THE AMERICAN BAR,
CASINO MUNICIPAL, NICE,
AND LATE OF THE
EMBASSY CLUB, LONDON

UNUSUAL TRIBES:
THE LLAMBRES OF PERU

IN A SMALL VILLAGE on the outskirts of Cuzco in Peru, there exists a curious strain of creature known as the Llambre. The word is a mixture of the Spanish words 'Llama' and 'hombre' (man). These half-man half-llamas are the result of interbreeding between humans and their livestock during the 17th century. The lower part of the llambre's body is recognisably human, being a two-legged upright animal with two arms and opposing thumbs. But the neck is elongated and covered with a thick pelt of wool, and the head is distinctly llama-like, with large eyes sitting either side of a long snout.

The llambres are gentle, though shy creatures, and tend to keep well away from humans and llamas, in spite of being close relatives to both species. The llambre's fur is much sought-after by the local Indians, who fashion it into very attractive and expensive waistcoats, and it commands much higher prices on the black market than regular llama wool. The llambres avoid relations with llamas because, although those creatures are irresistibly drawn to them, the llambre, like the mule, is completely infertile.

MYTHS & LEGENDS:
THE PIPELINES OF NUNCA

MYSTERY HAS SURROUNDED the existence of these enormous pipe-shaped lines, carved into the hills around Iquitos, since they were first discovered by Spanish Conquistadores in the 15th century. Extensive research among Inca folklore has revealed no indication about the possible origins or purpose of the lines. Some theories point to the existence of a pre-Inca people who worshipped the pipe as a sacred symbol, while others speak of the lines being the markings for an unusual species of ancient ball game. But the most popular theory among the local indigenous population is still more intriguing. They believe that the lines were carved into the earth for use as landing marks for alien spacecraft. Some locals even believe themselves to be the descendants of Venusian travellers, who marked the terrain so they could land their pipe-shaped spaceships and found secret colonies in the chosen land, Peru.

MYTHS & LEGENDS:
THE DEBONAIR DOLPHIN

THE INDIGENOUS TRIBES that inhabit the shores of the Amazon have many curious myths concerning the pink dolphin, or bufeo. The dolphin is perceived as a semi-divine being by some communities, while others regard it as an untrustworthy witchdoctor. One community believes that the dolphin's ear grants longevity from the favours of Priapus, while its grated left eye is considered an aphrodisiac powder. The most popular story, passed through generations of Amazon Indians since centuries ago, goes that the pink dolphins live in an underwater city in Lake Caballococha, downriver from Iquitos, near the Peru-Colombia border. By day the dolphins splash about in the river in a perfectly unremarkable manner, but at night they take on a slightly more advanced role in society. The bufeo transforms itself into a suave, silver-tongued gentleman dressed in a white linen suit and Panama hat, and spends the evening ambling about the Amazon villages seducing local ladies. Unwanted pregnancies within Indian communities are blamed on this magical animal, which unsurprisingly makes a frequent appearance on the local dinner table.

Los Angeles, USA, 12th October

I am seated at the oversized, imitation oak veneer escritoire of our room at the Radisson Beverly Pavilion, still reeling from the shock of our arrival in this appalling city. We have traversed arid deserts, navigated fetid swampland, fled from armed militia and entered the very heart of Babylon, yet nothing could have prepared us for Los Angeles. This vast, seemingly endless metropolis is entirely constructed of concrete, glass and steel; the avenues are rarely less than six lanes deep; the pedestrian and the smoker share the same social status as the petty criminal, and the natives devote most of their time to shouting at one another or sounding their klaxons.

After our many hazardous voyages, I had imagined an airline journey to be a straightforward exchange of funds in return for a comfortable seat, some choice aeroplane nosh and a glass or two of champagne while observing the passing clouds through the portals. Nothing could have been further from the reality of travelling in steerage with Aeroperu, in the company of a man on the outer edges of madness.

Iquitos had been a welcome respite after the ravages of our 2000-mile journey up the Amazon. Masaki took some excellent daguerreotypes of me in front of a bandstand designed by Alexandre Gustave Eiffel, and we admired the beautiful Portuguese glazed tiles that adorn many of the majestic buildings in the main plaza, built on the profits of the 1860s rubber boom. The funds from Victor's single-handed interior organ boom meant that we could afford to dine in the city's finest restaurants, and it was in one of these that the trouble started. We had just finished some delicious pink dolphin steaks in the Café de la Antiguedad, when the waiter delivered a couple of glasses of a curious green liquid that we hadn't ordered. The drink had a thick, gloopy consistency, and plumes of smoke were rising from it. "How strange," I remarked, "perhaps a local custom, to provide a complimentary warm digestif?"

Victor, never one to question the provenance of a free

drink, downed his glass in one while I inspected mine.
I looked to him for the appraisal of a connoisseur, but
instead of discussing the beverage's palette, nose and
finish, his response was to clutch his throat and
splutter. I was on the point of calling for a doctor,
when we were approached by a most singular fellow.

Almost naked save for some feathers dangling
strategically before his nether regions, his head was
adorned with a curious headdress constructed from a
distressed top hat with feathers and bones sticking out
of it. The man's eyes blazed in a quite alarming way,
the like of which I have not seen since the time my
Uncle Ernest was given a glass of wine spiked with LSD
in the sixties, and came to bid me goodnight in my cot,
stark naked except for a posy of begonias. "Me Kanuka,"
the man introduced himself, "Kanuka have your friend's
secrets. Your friend need Kanuka's secrets."

This didn't strike me as a particularly intelligent
piece of reasoning, but by now Victor was beginning to
foam at the mouth rather unattractively. Mainly for fear
of staining my immaculate linen suit did I take up
Kanuka's offer. "Come with me, follow Kanuka!" he
shrieked, bounding into the street and darting down an
alleyway. Masaki and I dragged Victor along behind him,
eventually ending up outside a corrugated iron shack on
the outskirts of the city. I peered into the dark
interior and could just about make out Kanuka's blazing
eyes flashing in a corner. "Inside, bring bring!" he
screeched. Following his instructions, Masaki and I laid
Victor down on a filthy old mattress and watched Kanuka
place various artefacts around him.

Much later, we learned from Trubshawe that Kanuka was a
shaman, and had given Victor a drink called Ayahuasca, a
potent concoction used to induce hallucinations. For the
next five hours, Masaki and I sat in that smelly little
hut, as Kanuka guided Victor through a series of
mystical journeys on an entirely astral plane. All we
could see before us was a quivering, foaming, blabbering
buffoon on an old mattress, but from Victor's reports
many days later, we learned that he had been transformed
first into an Inca warrior, and in this guise had
communed with various spirit gods, married a Venusian

princess, established an intergalactic empire in 2,000 BC which he had ruled until a meteor destroyed it, then he had returned to earth and, after a brief stint as a man-eating jaguar, worked as a slave for the Spanish Conquistadores until a bout of leprosy forced him into early retirement.

When it was all over, we asked Kanuka why he had selected Victor as a candidate for his shamanistic practices. "This man drink Scotty whisky too much. Looking for answers. Ayahuasca give answers."

On the journey back to the hotel, Victor didn't strike me as a man who had many answers. He looked like someone with quite a few questions along the lines of "Who in the name of Beelzebub am I?" But there are very few conditions that cannot be cured with a nice hot bath, a cup of strong tea and one of Masaki's vigorous massages.

We cut short our stay in Iquitos, and took the next Aeroperu flight to the USA. The flight took eight hours, during which time we were given one small bowl of lukewarm guinea pig stew and one glass of chicha, a revolting brew made from the yucca plant. My, those Peruvians really know how to live. Victor was not in a fit state to notice the victuals, since Ayahuasca has various hazardous side effects for the Western palate, one of them being chronic nausea and vomiting. The other quality that made him a less than ideal airline companion was his habit of breaking into sudden bursts of the Ancient Inca language, and staring wildly at the stewardess when she asked him if he wanted anything, with the response: "I want your kidneys."

AMERICAN PIE

THE AMERICANS PRIDE themselves on their food, and it is worth studying their excellent variety of cuisine to enjoy it to its fullest, as the Americans do. Here are some of the most typical dishes:

PIZZA: A large triangle of dough sold on street corners, with a thin layer of tomato paste and a couple of cheese gratings. Not to be confused with the Italian dish of the same name.

HAMBURGER: For some Americans this meat patty in a bread roll with salad and ketchup is a meal in itself, while for others it is a snack to be taken between meals.

SALT BEEF BAGEL: Reflecting the rich cultural diversity of the Americans, this dish is similar to the hamburger, except that the bun has a hole in it and the meat is kosher.

PRETZEL: When we British leave our bread in the bread bin for too long, it goes hard and we throw it away. Waste not, want not, say the Americans! They decorate it with sesame seeds and serve it on street corners. "Great with alcohol-free beer!" – President Bush.

APPLE PIE: Not merely a foodstuff for the Americans, but more of a sacrament. Every time an American eats a slice of apple pie, he or she is transported back to the magical days of their childhood. As you will note on your travels, many Americans had unforgettable childhoods.

ICE CREAM: If the word conjures an image of a delicate slice of Cassatta served with a single wafer, then be prepared for a surprise. Amercian ice cream comes in a bucket with a large wooden shovel to eat it with. Typical flavours are peanut butter and cheese, and raw cookie dough.

Los Angeles Enquirer

October 16 / Evening Edition   Vol. XXI Edition No. 12,172 Price 50c

Scientists Discover Gene for Panache

Los Angeles, 14th October:
American scientists have announced yet another amazing advance in the mapping of the human genome when they identified the gene said to be responsible for panache.
Carl Bogdanovich reports.

The gene believed to be responsible for panache when observed under an electron microscope

Up until now, scientists had thought that panache might be an acquired characteristic, usually the result of reading poetry, being acquainted with a very good tailor or the excessive consumption of rare malt whisky, but now they believe that there is possibly one gene or a small sequence of genes that predetermine whether a man or woman is likely to exhibit panache, savoir faire or suaveness.

Researchers were initially intrigued by the uneven distribution of panache across the globe. It is a rare condition in the United States of America and is mainly found in concentrated pockets in Europe, India, Turkey and Singapore. Englishmen are particularly susceptible to the condition and many theories have been put forward suggesting that cases might be due to education, dietary or climatic factors.

In an article published in this month's *Science Now*, Professor

Truman Finkelberger of the California Institute for Gene Research, states that "previous theories that dismissed panache as a minor affectation of the effete upper class Englishman have now been blown out of the water. Detailed research has revealed that even children born to lower middle class families in the UK can be blessed with impeccable manners."

Equipped with this information, Professor Finkelberger set to work to discover the reasons behind the relative dearth of panache across the US when compared to similar groups in the United Kingdom and across Europe. What he discovered has rocked the world of science. "The small amount of cases of panache found in the United States is not, as was previously thought, due to fast food consumption and a general erosion of normal standards

of civilised behaviour, but is in fact a product of genetic mutation. In most Americans the gene for panache has mutated into a recessive, and is only made manifest when two recessive gene carriers have offspring."

Further research reveals that John Malkovich, Clark Gable and Dorothy Parker are among the rare American citizens who have displayed the characteristics of fully blown panache. Interviewed in his Nantucket pied-a-terre, Mr Malkovich commented: "Since early childhood I've felt sure that sooner or later science would come up with a plausible explanation for my innate languidity."

Houston, USA, 28th October

After my little encounter in Peru with that Ayahuasca concoction I was somewhat peeved to discover that Gustav had not invested in a case of the stuff. It would surely have come in useful to distract our attention from the dreadful vulgarity of L.A.

Thankfully we have now relocated to the Belvedere Royale Hotel in Houston, which has put us in a far more sanguine state of mind, although to my tastes the building is a bit too giddyingly tall for complete comfort. Gustav and I have a suite of rooms on the 158th floor and if it weren't for a medicinal dose of gin and tonic every time I negotiate the lift I'm sure I'd be in the final stages of altitude sickness by now.

Back in Los Angeles, to add insult to ennui, Masaki had unimaginatively insisted that we should travel by that most public of Public Transport, the Greyhound Bus on our journey from "The City of Angels" to "Space City". The usual protests resulted and the usual denouement ensued.

As expected, public transport turned out to be gruesome, but initially not as gruesome as we had feared. We put Masaki to work, instructing him to construct a species of Bedouin tent from our travel kilims. He skilfully strung up the cloth so as to completely enclose our seats, suspending a pitched roof with string from the coach skylight and illuminating the interior with decorative oil lamps that we had acquired along the way. Whilst Masaki set to work with his primus stove on the rear seat preparing some French toast and devilled kidneys, I pursued that Holy Grail of the refined drinker, endeavouring to mix three of the finest Dry Martinis ever made. Meanwhile, Gustav settled down and busied himself with a new toy he had purchased from a tobacconist in Los Angeles: a large Meerschaum pipe equipped with a catalytic converter that purported to sidestep the draconian anti-smoking laws that seemed to mar the west coast of America.

Our hermetic concealment from fellow passengers may have shielded us from the unpleasant habits of the common man, but had also kept us ignorant of the fact that at each stop along the way the coach had been gradually filling up. By the time the bus had reached Tucson the only "spare" seats available were those adjacent to Masaki, Gustav and myself. Shortly after the coach had moved away from the curb, our kilim was roughly pulled from the ceiling and a large ugly-looking man plonked himself haphazardly down in the seat next to Gustav.

"Not crashin' yer lil' pardy now, am I?" he slurred, clearly drunk. "My name's Dwight. I'm fresh outta whisky, you guys got some liquor?"

Gustav blinked, clearly horrified. Closer inspection of our new acquaintance confirmed to my mind that my colleague's reaction was wholly justified. His head was not dissimilar to one of the Chesterfield sofas found in the Sheridan, the colour of ox-blood, but with eyes, nose and mouth standing in for where the buttons ought to be. To relieve the monotony of the upholstery theme he had contrived somehow to acquire an impressive scar, which started from just above the left eye and continued down to the corner of his mouth. His head was shaven and he was wearing a baseball cap.

"My c-colleague, Victor is immensely fond of malt whisky and has quite a bit stashed away behind us. M-maybe you would care to join him and swap a few stories or something or other ..." attempted Gustav, but Dwight just stared a stare of vacant menace for a few seconds before continuing.

"Hey, Victor, why don't you just hand me through one of those bottles of whisky now?"

I acquiesced swiftly, trying not to make too many sudden moves in the process.

"Y'see after 21 years in the state penitentiary a man gets kinda thirsty ... I'm not sayin' I didn't deserve it, but when some guy steals your woman he better believe that you ain't gonna take it lyin' down ..."

From this point and for the next two hours, Dwight went on to regale us with hair-raising tales of wringing men's necks "like cotton-pickin' turkeys" and how "a cheatin' woman" is no better than "a goddam whore". He then spent a good 45 minutes detailing the damage that can be inflicted upon the human head using motorised farmyard implements.

Gustav, who had had enough after the first seven seconds, sat carefully rigid throughout his ordeal, nodding politely or issuing a strangulated "Oh really?" whenever it seemed appropriate. By the time we had reached El Paso, Dwight had fallen into a drunken coma. His gargantuan head was firmly lodged on Gustav's shoulder, pinning my colleague against the window and liberally weeping viscous saliva over his lapel.

Gustav communicated with me out of the corner of his mouth through the gap in the seats: "This ape is drowning me in mucus. Something has to be done".

"It's OK," I replied in a whisper. "Masaki seems to have a splendid plan."

While we had been engaged in polite conversation with Dwight, the coach had cleared out somewhat and Masaki had noticed that the empty seat opposite also doubled up as the fire exit.

I wandered nonchalantly over to the exit and took firm hold of the release mechanism. Meanwhile Masaki prodded Dwight back into wakefulness.

"Er, Mr Dwight, take that you big brute," he shouted, grimacing horribly and giving him a tremendous poke in the eye. Dwight roared into action in a nanosecond, lashing out at Masaki with fists the size of hams.

"Come an' get me, you goddam mother!" I had no idea where Masaki picked up this sort of language, but it definitely had the desired effect. Dwight obligingly rushed at Masaki who performed a highly agile side step, leaving Dwight to vacate the bus through the now open emergency door. As we looked through the back window we could see him kicking up quite a lot of dust as he rolled down the side of the road and into a cactus thicket.

Gustav dabbed his ruined jacket with a lavender-scented handkerchief. "If you'd only thought of that six hours ago," he observed with a note of weariness in his voice.

Vic Darkwood

V A D

Victor Agamemnon Darkwood Esq.
Suite 17, The Sheridan Club, St. James's, London SW1

Bill Gates,   Belvedere Royale Hotel,
Chairman,   Prairie Boulevard,
Microsoft Corporation,   Houston
Redmond, Washington, USA

29th October

Dear Mr Gates,

My colleague Gustav Temple and I have been traversing this fine country of yours for just over a week now and during the course of our wanderings we have been hearing your name with some regularity.

The "word on the street" has it that you are the "bee's knees" when it comes to a fiendishly clever contrivance called the "personal computer". Unfortunately neither of us have the foggiest understanding about this technological mallarky, but we have heard that such pastimes are all the rage with the so-called "youth" of America. Not to appear 'stick in the mud' we thought that we should maybe make a few enquiries to see what all the ballyhoo is about.

To cut to the chase, we hear that you provide a service called the Internet Explorer. As we have absolutely no intention of exploring the damned thing ourselves, we had hoped you might be able to get one of these internet explorer johnnies of yours to look up a few "sites" on our behalf. Gustav and I are rather intrigued to discover the contents of an avant-garde Swedish arthouse cinema site called www.mistresslegume.com. In addition, Gustav would be much obliged if you could ask the fellow, while he's at it, to look up any sites that might specialise in 16th century enamel Limoges funerary urns of which he is tremendously fond.

Finally, I have also been told that Berry Bros & Rudd of St. James have a web site from which fine wines and vintage port may be purchased mail order and dispatched throughout the globe. Can this possibly be true?

Cordial regards

Vic Darkwood

Microsoft Corporation
Redmond, Washington, United States of America
e: microsoftsquillions.com

30th October,

Dear Mr Darkwood,

We regret to inform you that Mr Gates is unable to respond directly to queries of this nature.

Please refer to your Microsoft stockist for information on current products.

Yours sincerely

Jed Wallinger

P.S. Our local law enforcement agency have expressed an interest in interviewing you with regard to www.mistresslegume.com

LET'S SPEAK HIP-HOP

THE AMERICAN MUSIC INDUSTRY has produced a peculiar language all of its own. Should you find yourself in one of the more "colourful" parts of town, the following phrases will assist you to hold your own among the "homeys in the hood".

Ay yo trip, check out my b-boy rhyme and riddle.
Hello there old fellow, would you like me to read you some of my poetry?

My seven bizzos got boo-yaa bling bling.
I always ensure that my numerous mistresses are generously decorated with the finest jewels.

Yo, let's dip to the mall.
I've got a spiffing idea – let's go and do some shopping!

Now I gotta wetcha cos you dissed ma honey.
I'm afraid I shall have to demand satisfaction in response to the aspersions you have cast on my ladylove.

Cause some of y'all niggas is bitches too.
It cannot be denied that the population is roughly divided into equal amounts of ladies and gentlemen.

I'm an addict for sneakers, 20's of cheeba and bitches with beepers.
There is nothing more pleasant, in my view, than some lovely plimsolls, a delicious jazz cigarette and the company of an attractive lady friend.

SARTORIAL CONFUSION

WHILE MANY AMERICANS can be every bit as elegant as the British, and the larger US cities often boast bespoke tailors and quality department stores, confusion may occasionally arise over terminology. The Americans' language is superficially identical to British English, but beware of differences in meaning between similar sounding words. A "pissed fag", for example, would be a meaningless English expression describing a drunken cigarette, while in America it would be an accurate description of an irate homosexual. Similar confusion can arise on a visit to Brooks Brothers, so I have provided a handy guide to American tailoring terms and their British equivalents.

Vest	Waistcoat
Pants	Trousers
Suspenders	Braces
Derby hat	Bowler hat
Baseball cap	No British equivalent
Rhinestone-studded jumpsuit	No British equivalent
Shorts, Hawaiian shirt, Stetson, cowboy boots	Pantomime outfit
Velour leisurewear, gold jewellery, hearing aid	Flat cap, muffler, Jack Russell
Vera Wang dress, Jimmy Choo mules, Luis Vuitton bag, Botox, collagen, silicone	Topshop dress, white stilettos, fake Luis Vuitton bag, wrinkles, cigarette, wonderbra
Plaid shirt, jeans, racoon hat, boots, axe	Overalls, tweed cap, Wellington boots, tractor

London, England, 1st November

Ah, the many and varied joys of travel! They can only be fully appreciated from one's favourite armchair in the Smoking Room of the Sheridan Club, surrounded by adoring acquaintances listening raptly to one's tales while constantly replenishing one's glass with vintage Armagnac. Arbuthnot and Wilkinson made for a very interesting study in opposing forces. The former, having £20,000 in his pocket to confirm his undying faith in us, was positively radiant with joy, the glow from his cheeks casting a pleasant rosy hue over the club members clustered around our chairs.

Wilkinson, conversely, was a dark presence by the fireplace, fuming with rage at being proved entirely wrong about myself and Mr Darkwood's capabilities. The decent thing to do would have been a discreet withdrawal from the premises, having settled our bill with the management. Yet Wilkinson was clearly drawn to our tales, much as a defeated and bloodied pugilist would derive a morbid fascination from hearing every detail of his opponent's winning technique.

And what tales we had to impart, as you well know, dear reader! But allow me, if you will, to take your mind back to the events leading up to the final and, as it turned out, the most extraordinary leg of the entire journey.

Houston, being the capital of the so-called Lone Star State, had a perverse charm about it that had been entirely absent in Los Angeles. The patent absurdity of grown men walking about with enormous Stetson hats appealed to us, as did the occasional sight of a man trotting along a busy highway on horseback. There was something almost Victorian about it, despite the rather crude denim garments sported on the Texans' lower bodies. Moving about the city in search of a new mode of transport was no easy matter, for everywhere we went a large crowd of youths would gather around us, asking us whether we were Sherlock Holmes or James Bond. When we patiently explained that these were merely fictional characters, they became further confused, and we found it easier to simply agree with them.

Thus it was that James Bond (myself), Sherlock Holmes (Victor) and Fu Manchu (Masaki) spent a fruitless four days in Houston trying to find a new form of transport to take us back to England. We had used up every vehicle capable of taking us on the final transatlantic leg of the journey. Even Masaki's mind had gone as blank as his facial expression. There were no more "leaping salmon" or "blind serpents" issuing from his stock of aphoristic travel advice.

It was an article in a newspaper that finally provided a solution. "Challenger VII to launch Thursday", screamed, or rather muttered, the headlines. A space shuttle was the only form of air transport that we had not yet used, and it being Thursday, we caught the next bus to Houston Space Station. Security was naturally very tight, and the closest we were able to get to the shuttle was to observe it being prepared through the thick glass of the viewing platform.

When a delay was announced, Masaki, ever the opportunist, led us out of the viewing platform and into the fields surrounding the take-off zone. Some unknowable instinct seemed to be driving the inscrutable one, and having no better ideas of our own, we complied with his instructions to settle in a field not far from the shuttle. We spent the evening assisting Masaki to construct an unusual and seemingly pointless mound of earth. By nightfall he was still digging about like a man possessed, piling handful after handful of earth onto the mound, until it bore a rather crude likeness to St James's Palace.

Victor and I soon tired of the whole business and went to sleep, he curled up in his greatcoat and I in my thickest pair of winceyette pyjamas and a woollen dressing gown from Turnbull & Asser. I carefully hung my Tommy Nutter striped blazer and cream moleskins on the outside of my travelling trunk in order to air them for the following day, placing my straw boater, Malacca cane and yellow kid leather gloves nearby.

We were awoken around four o'clock in the morning by some bright lights in the sky. As they became brighter, the three of us sat bolt upright in amazement. The lights were on the underside of a species of circular aircraft which appeared to be attempting to land some 30 feet from where we had made camp. By the time the craft had landed, with much hissing and whirring and flashing lights, the three of us were rooted to the spot with a mixture of expectancy and mild terror.

The whirring came to a stop. From the domed surface of what I now took to be a spaceship, a door opened and a set of steps was mechanically lowered. A voice came from within the interior: "Who is the proprietor of that charming blazer?" it said, with a voice remarkably like someone schooled at Eton.

"Um, er, well … it is I," I stammered, not even sure whether the creature I was addressing was humanoid.

"There is no finer maker of blazers than Mr Tommy Nutter," the voice continued, with, I noted, a degree of accuracy. "Please step into the craft, Mr –?"

"Temple," I replied. "Gustav Temple, at your service." I marched towards the spaceship with the confidence instilled by any discussion of quality raiment.

Inside, the craft was not as futuristic as I had expected. In fact, it reminded me of the old reading room of the British Library. Wood-panelled throughout, the fixtures and fittings were all nicely aged brown leather in the late Victorian style. The controls and navigating equipment seemed to be constructed from Bakelite and resembled antique radio equipment. Seated behind a set of screens set in polished walnut was the most extraordinary creature I have ever set eyes upon.

His body was clad in an immaculate three-piece worsted suit, with a pink shirt, a paisley tie and matching handkerchief in the breast pocket. All very well and good, but what a face! If a fluorescent yellow balloon had been fully inflated then suddenly burst, collapsing on itself in an untidy mass of wrinkles, it might resemble this remarkable visage. The other characters aboard the ship had similarly revolting features and all were dressed as elegantly as the man who had addressed me.

"Allow me to introduce myself," he said cordially. "I am Captain Zlatorog of the planet Arcadus. May I first of all reassure you that you and your friends are not in any danger. We are merely in search of civilisation and so far we seem to have had difficulty in finding it on this planet. May I secondly compliment you on your exquisite nightwear."

"Oh, this old thing," I replied. "Just a little caprice of Francis's at Turnbull & Asser, he knocked it up when he was making my winter shirts."

"Ah, Turnbull & Asser," said my interlocutor wistfully. "I wonder whether you would be so kind as to tell me where I can find them? We have searched this land high and low and have not come across the very thing we came all the way to earth for, namely to stock up on some new suits from Savile Row and purchase some victuals at Fortnum & Mason."

"But the places you mention are both in London, England, whereas we are in the USA, where tailors can be found, but not as you or I would know them."

"Excuse me? What is USA?"

Once I had explained the difference between Britain and America to Captain Zlatorog, he was eager to correct his navigation instruments and proceed at once to Blighty. "Please, bring your friends aboard and let us travel to civilisation!"

Masaki and Victor boarded the vessel and presently it lifted into the sky. We watched the flickering lights of Houston's thwarted space programme disappear, and soon we were on a direct course for London. The prospect of being home at last filled us with unparalleled joy, and Captain Zlatorog had his private secretary take notes as Victor and I discussed all the fine things we would do, once returned to the terra firma of SW1.

Some twelve hours later, having taken a brief detour to show us the sights of Mars (not much to see, really), the captain landed his spaceship in Hyde Park in the dead of night. We bid a fond farewell to Mr Zlatorog, inviting him to visit us at the club whenever he wished. I also gave him a letter of introduction to various Savile Row tailors, and Victor gave him the address of the exclusive supplier of Thedgeley's Old Cut Marmalade.

It was a long walk across the park to our rooms in Pimlico, but with Masaki bearing the luggage, the sensation of firm, green English soil under our feet was the most delightful of our entire voyage.

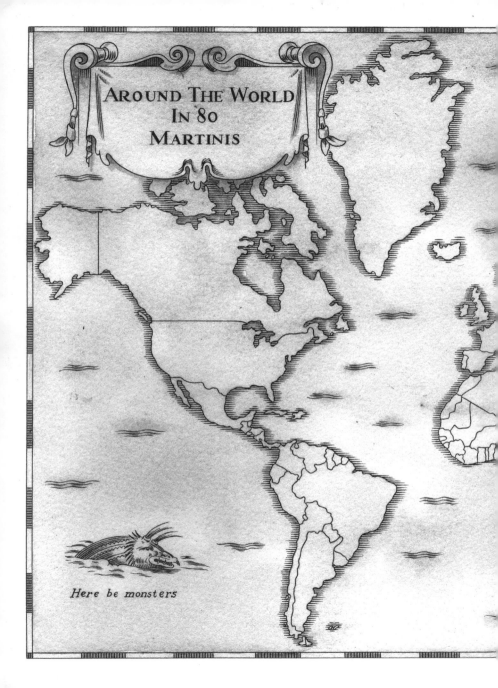

Here be monsters